One Womb Wound at a Time

POSTPARTUM JOURNAL

MRS. SHANTAY MCKENNIE

Thanks With Gratuity

I thank my ex-husband for showing me what it is and isn't to admit how stressed out becoming a parent can be. WIth our second daughter he had the toughest times because she is still such a momma's girl which is rare. He never failed at telling me how he couldn't handle her crying, how nothing he did soothed her and all she wanted was her momma and some damn titty milk. Had I not remembered those moments, I'm not sure I would have been able to admit how difficult it was for me and sometimes how difficult it still is for me to grow through those crying moments.

I thank my ex-fiance, & best friend, had he not chosen the actions he chose I wouldn't have been able to write this journal. It would've never come into existence. Most times it's the troublesome times that bring out the best and the worst in us. Now some may say that's bad that the worst side reveals itself, however I'm the different type of folk who admire one and those who can and are willing to release those inner demons and darker sides of themselves. People like myself. It's the darker sides and entities that give us the power to make good decisions and yes bad decisions in life. DO you want to feed the evil or the good? That's the answer we must always ask ourselves with every good and bad experience we have in life. Personally I will admit I did both! One day it was good and then another day it was bad, to me and for me that's normal because no one on this Earth in this realm is always good or always bad. Somehow and some way we all find or utilize the

1

balance within ourselves and our lives. I'm grateful to have that and to actually be able to acknowledge it, accept it, and practice it. Love has the most profound ways of making us grow whether we want or not, just like life.

I appreciate all the people I've met throughout this part of my journey and prior to for the knowledge and wisdom they were so happy to share with me. Being an adult has its challenges on it's own. But being an adult and raising a little person to become an adult is even more of a double challenge and to those with multiples at once not just back to back I commend you!

I wasn't quite sure how or what this would turn out to be, I just knew that I needed to do it for my own sake and sanity. I had to make it known, put it out in the open because it's such a hidden topic of discussion. Mothers are shamed for experiencing the smallest incline of postpartum depression. Fathers, fathers better not dare to even mention postpartum depression or they'll be laughed at just like they are for having emotions and expressing them. Postpartum is what aids in infant death rates, marital issues, mental problems, emotional trauma, parenting problems, and that's just the surface of it all. I'm not exactly sure who, what, when, where, how, or why postpartum is so frowned upon, and kept so quiet. However I do want to say that within the past few years there has been a rise in the attention it is getting and the care that is coming along with it.

Whatever part of the postpartum spectrum you are on (because there's such a huge spectrum like autism) please do not ever hide it or pretend that you are okay. Simple baby blues are some of the first signs of postpartum depression. Talk to your doctor, counselor, OBGYN, and/or midwife and yes even your doula. Never be afraid or ashamed to get help being a parent, we all need help in life.

Day 1

Healing Pains

The beauty of birth equates to the beauty in
healing from regular pains of life.

Beauty is pain

Life is pain

Healing is pain

They all are something we all will experience in some form, shape
or fashion.

My journey after child birth x5

#MotherOf5

#BirthDoula

#GlobalWoman

#WomanOfLife

#SpiritualLifeCoach

#NonToxicLife

#GlobalMom

#SexDoula

Affirm: I Am the Beginning and my ending is just as powerful and strong as my beginning.

How do you plan on finishing your journey? Knowing this will help you begin and "PUSH" through when it seems like it's too much for you to bear.

_____

_____

_____

_____

_____

_____

_____

_____

_____

_____

_____

_____

_____

Day 2

Affirm: I Am proud of myself and all that I have accomplished.

It isn't always easy to face this and acknowledge as a human being, especially as a mother and woman!

We're always pushing and striving for better and we are never stopping to say I did that or I'm happy with the smallest and simplest things. However, we can encourage others to do so.

As a mother, Doula, and woman. I encourage "MYSELF" and others to stop for a moment and just give yourself a huge hug, a pat on the back, and celebrate how outstanding you are. Within giving birth we see our birth story happening one way and sometimes it doesn't turn out the way we want or would like it to. Now in our minds we're thinking, "just let me do it so it's done right!" Being in the vulnerable state of labor doesn't always permit you to "do it yourself".

I can say this because I have 5 birth stories to share! Yes, five! When reality hits and you realize that sometimes you need help because things happen and you are just exhausted etc., it becomes very disheartening because as a mother, woman, wife, all you see is bringing your baby into this realm in the best way and the most loving way possible.

Dear me and star 🖋 mommies,

I want you to know that you have done more than the typical "I'll do it myself!"

You GAVE BIRTH!

That is far more vulnerable and powerful than anything on this planet or in this realm.

I love you and be proud of that accomplishment no matter what life may be.

#WomanOfLife

What is something powerful you can celebrate out loud about your labor and birth story?

Day 3

Mother Warrior

Sometimes it will feel like (and it really is) like we're doing it all alone! 😫😩😖

I recently read a post or comment on facebook that said, "Women are great multitaskers, we just don't have an option to choose if we want to do it or not." NEWSFLASH! "We don't have an option, it has toget done."

How bitter sweet is this!?

This isn't to put down men or fathers because trust me we know who the real daddies are! What this IS about though is the fact that a woman's mindset says, "when there's a will there's a way." Yesterday I mentioned how we always strive for the best and how we want nothing but the best welcoming into this realm for our babies. Today is similar with a little twist.

Do we want to get up, and do, and go, and be super mommy or warrior women?

Hell NOoooooooo sometimes we just don't want to do anything at all. And that includes mothering. Sometimes we don't feel well, we truly aren't capable or able. We need some time, some space, some peace of fuckin mind for heavens sake, shit!

But we make it look so simple and so easy like we are capable and able. 😩 no we're tired and achy, need a break and some tlc.

Sometimes we're just plain fed the fuck up with everything and everyone and sometimes that includes ourselves because we are the ones who tolerate this shit.

Yup it gets that deep all the curse words, all the emotions, the mentality, the spirit depletion and more. But by the time we reach this point, most times, we have worn ourselves thin as the Christmas tissue paper we use to decorate the gift bags. We do this because we love and we care. Because we choose to be more than what you bargained for. Because nurturing, and healing is what we do naturally. We strap on our big girl panties (the granny ones that are back in style now 😄) and we get shit done!

It isn't just for the sake of getting things done because without us nothing gets done. It's for the simple fact that regardless of daddy planting the seed for the family to grow. Mommy is the backbone of the family, this is her family, this is her pride and joy! This is what she lives for, what she fights for, what she breathes for, what she strives and lives for. This is her and she is it!

- So the next time you see a Mother Warrior pushing further and further, harder and harder than before. Give her a helping hand even if that means passing her her favorite color lipstick 💄◆ so she can brace the world happier, more gorgeous, and loved once more.

Day 4

You've been running for a while now Mother Warrior it's okay to stop for a moment and catch your breath.

#WomanOfLife

Affirm: This Shit IS Done Affirm: Mindfulness is not easy but it helps you breathe easier.

Today we played, we laughed, we fought (yes I fought with my 1 year old baby lol), he cried, I got upset, we went into separate corners of the room, we took a nap, etc.

Sounds like a married couple right 😂 well yes I agree it does.

As a mother you absolutely must find your gray area with children. Am I saying you need to allow them to get away with things? Nope, not at all.

What I Am saying is keep your sanity and learn to breathe and be mindful that your toddler has a different view on things than you do. It sounds like you're giving a child more than what's necessary but they have necessities, feelings, wants, and more just like adults do.

It's weird but laugh and be happy. I had fun finding the little things and the big things. One of my favorite lessons today other than us writing and that was hilarious lol. Was understanding why DoJo assumed me telling him no meant he couldn't have his mommy.

In his little smarter than average mind saying no means he can't have me or come to me because I have his new baby sister. So he resented her. Once I changed my vocabulary to hold on, wait a moment, come sit next to mommy, things of that nature he responded better because none of it meant he couldn't have me at all.

This little #SpiritOfDoJo is making me better and better as a person overall!

So grateful to be his mommy.

How can you be more mindful with your new person in this world?

_____

_____

_____

_____

_____

How can you be mindful of yourself through this journey?

_____

_____

_____

_____

_____

Day 5

I just love me some them! If I cry, you cry, we cry, together (Lil Mo & Ja Rule) lol!

No but seriously that's exactly how it is with these two tiny people that I have now. I remember doing this with Layla and Shiya and then Layla, Shiya, & Jr. But today was different. DoJo could sense that I didn't wanna go and do just like they didn't. Complimenting him went a longgggggggg way today. I'm upset because all day I kept saying he gets his favorite ice cream today. Here it is 11:35 pm and my baby boy is fast asleep holding onto his mommy and I didn't give him his ice cream!

He doesn't know that was on my mind and heart but I did/ do! I know, I know, don't beat yourself up mommy. This isn't easy for him at all because everyone in the house is big except for him. Then here comes someone smaller than him and needs a little more attention than he does, which really isn't the case because she likes to be left alone. But he knows she is smaller and he knows mommy is giving love to her like I have to him.

I want him to know I appreciate him being patient, and not crying because I couldn't get to him right away like I usually would be able to. I want him to know that he's still my baby boy even when he's being a big boy for someone so little (he's really a big boy in size, mind, and spirit). I want him to know that I don't love him any less because he has moments of not wanting SisSea to take his baby spot. I want him to know that I'm proud of all of his little accomplishments. I want DoJo to know that I'm so honored to be his mommy! I'm in love with being his mommy. This all may seem like little things and even unnecessary to some. But the truth is, being a mommy there will always be moments like this. Being a mommy to multiple children no matter the age is going to challenge you in ways you'd never imagine. These little, simple, unnecessary things are the things that will stress ANY "mother" out. Remember we only want what's best for our babies and giving them ice cream for an"ALL DAY ACCOMPLISHMENT" is one of the ways we can say thank you for being the best you can be, without losing what's left of us on that day.

Affirm: I Am doing the best that I Am Able to do at each moment.

What have you been beating yourself up about?

_____

_____

_____

_____

_____

_____

_____

_____

_____

_____

Look who got their favorite ice cream!

Sometimes I feel like, wait, I know children can sense when we mean and don't mean things. He knew

I wanted to reward him for being good so he took full advantage of it lol.

One thing is for sure he was happy to see daddy come home and so was I! My body was even more happy because everything I was holding together while he was gone (I had to be strong and push through things with my teenagers help and me by myself at times) came falling out and aching like I took off my waist trainer! Mommies and daddies, sisters, brothers, cousins, aunts, uncles, nieces, nephews, children ...

Day 6

All the family and friends that are able to jump in and help a mommy who has just given birth to a star. Please, do jump in and help as much as possible in whatever and however way you can.

Are there some mothers out there who will contest and claim they have it!? YES, ABSOLUTELY! They may have it and are able to get up and do and go. But honey, listen to me sis!

YOU ARE PROLONGING YOUR HEALING BY NOT RESTING AND HEALING!

I know from experience, this is baby for me and I in the past have been the I got this mother and was her at some point within the past week. It doesn't help you, you aren't proving anything except that you're hurting yourself more by not resting. It takes 30-45 days just for your body to be truly strong enough to get up and get going on SOME of your daily routines. So please sis and myself, TAKE THE HELP! Better yet ASK FOR THE HELP because it is "desperately and health wise ('mentally, physically, spiritually, and emotionally) needed.

I love you and be happy that love is shown through the help you are given!Affirm: Healing requires rest, I give myself permission to rest to heal and just because.

Make a list of things you want help with and are okay with asking for help, even if it's hard to ask, make the list anyways and leave it out for everyone to see. Don't be upset if no one does anything it's still your responsibility to ask..

1.

2.

3.

4.

5.

6.

7.

8.

9.

10.

11.

12.

13.

14.

15.

Day 7

Well it wasn't too bad in all honesty. I mean it was the weekend so I had help of course. We as a family (minus Jr. because he always runs upstairs to his room) watched a couple of movies and ate homemade nachos for lunch.

The more difficult parts come from learning and listening, understanding more of DoJo's perspective on this whole big brother thing. I swear if it was like this when Layla, Shiya, and Jr. were little and I didn't notice, then I truly, truly, truly apologize to my teenagers! Because I can see the sadness in his face, the irritation and more. I have to admit that today I realized that his reasons for crying more than he usually does is because he sees and hears SisSea crying and notices that we run to her, hold her, and more to help soothe her cries.

Now I know he isn't aware that he is reverting to more baby behavior that he has grown from. But I do see how stressful this can be when a child goes backwards. I also see how stressful it is for the baby/toddler to experience this message/signal being unintentionally sent. Somehow some way both the parent(s) have to come to a level of patience with themselves first because that's where the understanding lies. Then with the baby/toddler because they crave and need it from you the most. Only you can give them the comfort they are seeking through such a transition/adjustment in everyone's lives.

Tears of learning and love have shown me the most understanding, inner-standing and growth I could ever imagine.

You all may get tired of me sharing my growth as a parent through the #SpiritOfDoJo but this baby is the blessing a lot of people need in life.

Affirm: I Am patient with myself and then with my baby, I Am parenting and loving.

What have you been rushing as a new mommy? How can you be more patient as a mommy and woman?

_____

_____

_____

_____

_____

_____

_____

_____

_____

_____

_____

_____

_____

Day 8

Inner balance; outward peace and joy!

We all have the tendency to be our worst critics, and our biggest cheerleader which is great! That's the way it should be. Balanced.

Let's focus on the reality though. Most times the best thing we are to ourselves is negativity. We can and do pump ourselves full of all the bad and we even subtract the good we've acknowledged and praised in the past. Only further suppressing the true form of who we are inside. Being able to recognize that you are bashing and abusing yourself isn't easy. But embracing the fact that you don't know how to truly love yourself is so powerful. All of this to say give yourself some time and some space to gain a new you, or hold on to what is attempting to be taken away from you.

Give yourself the opportunity to find the right position in your journey/life. Give yourself some praise for at least having the ambition, determination, drive, and will power to push and do more than what is needed of and from yourself.

Don't beat yourself up because it isn't your time to shine. Buff yourself up so when it is time to shine you shine as bright as you are meant to!

This is meant to say you don't have to do more than what's expected of you and all that is expected is for you to rest and heal. YOU to be tended to for once.

DAY 8

Affirm: I receive tender love and care with gratitude and ease. I Am worth the TLC my mind, body, spirit, and soul desires.

What does TLC look like to you?

_____

_____

_____

_____

_____

_____

_____

_____

_____

_____

_____

_____

_____

_____

Day 9

Patience, what little patience

The valuable lesson learned today ... "patience with yourself".

With all that you do as a being within this universe. Be patient with yourself. Patience helps us breathe and get through things we may feel is just too much to achieve or manage at the time. Remember how much you had to have through conceiving, pregnancy, labor, and birth!? You're going to need a lifetime of that going forward with life overall.

For me the thing to remember is not everything happens swiftly and more importantly, nothing legendary is built or achieved in haste.

Wanting to achieve the ultimate goal you've set for yourself is great. But wanting it to happen now! Well now, lol, I'll be the first to tell you it's better to just take your time or better yet the time intended for it all to happen from beginning to current to end.

In the words of my sistars "Trust THE ENTIRE Process. Even when the process seems like it is NOT working.

My trouble is it's hard for me to just sit and do nothing. I need to accomplish something, otherwise to me, I'm not living. Nine days and here I Am thinking and actually attempting to work from home in my business after just having a baby. A baby toddler and a newborn. Now you and I both know these babies are not in sync yet and they may never be in sync. But for me to put so much on myself in this short amount of time is insane. It's beautiful to see where my children's determination comes from. But it's bad because that means I'm not resting and causing my own demise. I'm looking for something and forcing something to happen that obviously is seeking and craving my patience and that something/someone includes these two little babies of mine and myself included.

Word to wise from the "wise". Be patient with yourself mommies! You will get there, you will get where you desire to be when you are destined to be there.

Affirm: Patients will keep you right on time, Divine Timing.

How much stress will you gain by allowing things to divinely take their place in life?

_____

_____

_____

_____

_____

_____

_____

_____

_____

_____

Day 10

Mother Daughter Ritual

In preparation for the moon and these special numbers that are attached with it. I've been quite excited to give #SisSea her first bath. Her first moon bath. Her first spiritual bath. Her first feminine bath.

I'm sharing just a little bit, but not too much. Now this isn't for everyone because these are mother to daughter spiritual intentions. What works for us may not work for you and your daughter. Feel free to use this info, but also feel free to change it to fit your desires as well.

We are doing a jar of tap water in the moonlight.

Some flowers of our choice. You may use what ones you desire.

They can be fresh for the bath or they can sit in the water in the moonlight overnight.

An essential oil of (y)our choice Some herbs of (y)our choice Candles of (y)our choice.

This can be a combined bath with you and your daughter(s) or you can bathe separately, it all depends on your intuition.

When finished bathing you can keep some of the ingredients and place them in a jar for keepsake, you can get rid of it all, or do whatever you choose with it. While in the bath you can read her, her first story, sing her her first song or chant her first incantation.

You can even meditate or play binaural beats. Something to hold with her for the rest of her human experience.

The purpose of the bath is to welcome your daughter to this realm with peace, love, light, and protection. To help aid and guide her throughout her life's journey and her life path's purpose.

Blessings to you and her/them

Mystical, Magickal, love, from a mother to her daughter

Day 11

So by this time last year I had already started taking my placenta capsules. Man when I tell you those things work! THEY WORK!

I kept her placenta and cord. I just haven't decided what I want to do with it. The cord I know what I'm going to do but not sure about her placenta. I hate that I had to freeze it but I did.

Now why do they work? Uhm the mood swings of releasing all of those pregnancy hormones is real! It's like going cold turkey! 🤯♀ I found myself about to cry, for what? Who knows lol 😄! I found myself extremely excited but I knew why lol. I found myself tired and exhausted knowing why but damn! All at once these emotions came flooding me. I decided early in the day I would do a before and after picture of me getting dressed. Sister, Girl, Honey 🍯, Child!

My before looks better than my after 😄😄😄😄😄. Good thing I have some essential oils and I'm eating healthy foods (when I'm not chasing down chocolate 🍫 chip 🍪 cookies), or I'll have a smoothie to combat this postpartum stuff!

Since I've taken the initiative to document daily as much as possible. I'm learning that this series isn't a choice, not that I ever thought it was. But what I am saying is "No matter what you have to go through these phases." The phases of your body detoxing from pregnancy in all forms, shapes, and fashions.

Now for the mommies who like me were pregnant back to back or who had multiples I'm imagining and experiencing this being even more intense because your body has so much more to rid itself of.

Postpartum is so fuckin real y'all!

But let's keep going and get through it because I have you all and you all have me!

Affirm: The Woman I Am Becoming is stronger than the woman I Am Freeing myself of.

Belly binding, tinctures, placenta capsules, sleep, water, a healthy diet, yoga, meditation, massages, and some amazing body butters are great ways to handle postpartum stresses. Counseling, sister circles, family and friends are great POWER sources to have. Sometimes a little more support is required. It does NOT make you weak or less of a woman and mother.

Day 12

Siblings syncing

So with every child you bear they have to learn and grow with each other. For a while I was rushing the process of these two little people #DoJoNSisSea to sync and get on a schedule together so I can adjust and move better as an individual, a mommy, wife, business woman and more!

Listen, be careful what you rush and what you ask for.
Yes they synced lol 😄
They stayed up until 2:00 a.m. together!
They cried together
They both were in my arms/lap, TOGETHER!
They were weirded out, nervous, & afraid of each other in my arms and lap together!
They wanted to be cuddled and calmed by me only, together!
They fell asleep in my arms/lap with me rocking them together!
Well damn, all of that!? Yes! Absolutely!
Any woman/mother would and could go insane or into manic depression after that all at once. Hell, I don't know a man that can handle that and not break a sweat 😅 lol.
Yes, some of you parents do it with ease but that doesn't mean the ones that struggle aren't giving it their best shot. Parenting is

about patience and mindfulness. Take the time to stop and breathe for yourself so you can jump back in it. Breathing creates a calm mind, body, and spirit! Take a moment to be mindful of not just yourself but others, primarily the little people. But after you've been patient and mindful enough to acknowledge that you're at your wits end!

Being mindful creates the mind space for us to see things from a different angle, perspective and perception. To know that there are more people and energies involved than just our own. Being mindful creates the opportunity for us to take a better course of action. None of this happens if you aren't leveled out first mommies, daddies, caretakers, sisters, brothers, aunts, uncles, nieces, nephews, family, & friends. Baby responds to you and your energy, and your body as well. So whatever you think you're hiding will be brought into the light by baby. Take a deep breath, soon you'll be handling this like you were built specifically for it and your baby. Because you were and you are created for this journey and your baby.....

Affirm: My Baby and I were created for each other.

Day 13

Enjoy the peace within yourself being a mommy. Sometimes we do so much and we fight with that on the inside. So much can feel like not enough at times. Not enough feels like I need to do more than I already am doing and more than I Am able to do.

I don't have a long story to share this time. Just some advice to~;~

Enjoy your inner peace when you have it. It's Yours and yours only unless you decide to share it with others or include them in your inner peace. Just don't forget to protect your peace at all cost

What brings you peace?

_____

_____

_____

What brings you peace as a woman?

_____

_____

_____

What brings you peace as a mother?

_____

_____

_____

Who and/or what adds to your peace or is worthy of sharing/being in your peace?

_____

_____

_____

In what way(s) can/do you protect your peace?

_____

_____

_____

Your Peace is your safe haven, it's sacred, it's powerful, it's who you are in your best & worst moments.

_____

_____

_____

_____

Day 14

Alone

That word can seem scary when you don't want to be alone or you've never been alone and even when you're always alone. Better yet when you shouldn't be alone. But this time mommies, I challenge you to think a little different about the word alone and being alone.

Being alone has so many benefits!

Alone to not have to monitor someone else and the way they move or do things.

Alone so you don't have to be in someone else's energy or space.

Alone so it's just you and your baby no one in between.

Alone so when the baby rests you have time just for you!

So yes take the help but also take a moment to be in your own space, mind, body, and spirit.

Alone is sometimes the best place to be. It's even better when it's meant for you to be alone.

Is it hard for you to be alone with yourself? If yes, why?

_____

_____

_____

DAY 14

Is it hard for you to be alone with your baby/babies? If yes, why?

_____

_____

_____

Do you ever feel like you will harm yourself or your baby/babies? If yes, why (Please seek professional help)?

_____

_____

_____

Who do you trust the most with this information and to help you with yourself and your baby/babies?

_____

_____

_____

Affirm: It is okay for me not to be okay.

Knowing when I Am NOT okay or okay to be alone by myself or alone with my baby/babies helps me be open enough to getting better with myself and being alone with my baby/babies.

I Am Worthy of Healing

Day 15

In asking and finding help during this time in life you have to first remember and then accept that

NOT EVERYONE WANTS TO HELP YOU.

So don't feel like shit or get angry because someone isn't willing to help in the smallest way. But do appreciate that they are honest enough to show or say they do not want to help, or they aren't able to help. At the very least you have their honesty. Respect and honesty go great in any and all relationships.

How~ever!

Truth be told, respect and honesty go a lot further when you have genuine help. That let me help you relax and rest type of help

Be glad you didn't get half ass help! That's worse than no help at all depending on your level of ocd. One thing I've learned along the journey of being a mother is not all people like children, babies. If you don't like children and/or babies then I don't want your help in that department at all. Those types of people and the people who half ass because they don't want to, don't know how and ain't tryna learn how are crossed off of my Ask For Help List.

Not all help is good help. Not all help is warranted help. Not all help is help you want or feel is necessary. Not everyone is meant to help even if they can and are able and willing. The help that is meant for you to have, will be available with ease and always right there waiting when you have to reach out and ask or grab it.

Hold on sis, mommy, Help is on the way.

Day 16

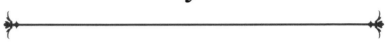

You got this mommy!

You've done more than just manage, you've done it all this time so keep doing it and don't forget to stop and breathe for yourself sometimes.

What do you want to be better at?

_____

_____

_____

_____

_____

_____

_____

_____

What do you want to be over so you don't have to stress about it anymore?

_____

_____

_____

_____

What actions if there are any can you take to help nurture the process?

_____

_____

_____

_____

_____

Is it something you can change without causing problems to yourself or your baby?If yes, How? If not, then why are you worried about it?

_____

_____

_____

_____

_____

Day 17

Yes, it gets hectic especially when you go out in public!

The best advice I have to give is to do things during their awake time. Nobody wants to do things when they're sleepy and cranky. Do you want to do things when you're sleepy?

Absolutely not!

So I'm sure the little people don't either. Make your life a little easier by working around their eating and resting times. But do know that time wears off fast.

I love you and keep being awesome.

Please be mindful that not everyone is able to handle what being a mommy really entails. Crying, bathroom stops, food, sleepiness, and more. Especially being all these things and having ALL of these moments in public. I've learned that being a mommy in general and especially in public means you're always under someone's watching eye whether you want to be, care to be or not. There will always be someone turning up their nose and making smart remarks, left handed compliments, challenging your mothering/parenting skills. Then there are those who are just genuine loving people that want to see you win even if it;s calming a fussy baby. There are those who will pitch in and help you because they know what parenting and being a mommy is all about. Hell they can see, and know what being a woman is all about. My point is to put your rhino skin

36

on when you step out of the comfort of your own home and even when you invite people into the comfort of your home. Know that it will ALWAYS be someone with something to say both good and bad. Sometimes it's worthwhile to listen because there is always something to learn about and an experience to learn from no matter the quality of the person, place, thing, or experience. Take what's meant for you to take and bear down momma and Push through the rest.

How was your day?

_____

_____

_____

_____

_____

_____

_____

_____

_____

_____

_____

_____

Day 18

THIS, is a breastfeeding 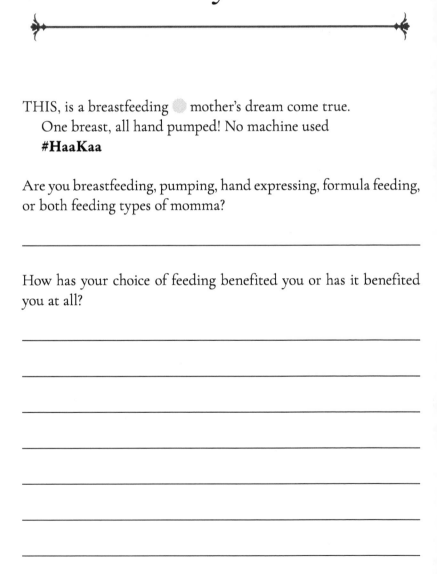 mother's dream come true.
One breast, all hand pumped! No machine used
#HaaKaa

Are you breastfeeding, pumping, hand expressing, formula feeding, or both feeding types of momma?

_____

How has your choice of feeding benefited you or has it benefited you at all?

_____

_____

_____

_____

_____

_____

_____

Is there anything you would change or need help with?

_____

_____

_____

_____

_____

_____

_____

_____

_____

_____

_____

_____

_____

_____

_____

Day 19

There is so much that plays a role into how postpartum either affects you and how you keep from letting it affect you.

I mean things like Circumstances, Situations, Food, Emotions, Colors, Thoughts, Feelings, The way people treat you.

The way you treat people, Music, The weather, Even clothes can trigger something or counteract the trigger to something positive. There's no definitive way to say yes it is postpartum and no it isn't. It's something like autism, it's such a wide spectrum.

My point is we don't know what is and what isn't postpartum because it affects us all differently. What we do know is the more life you consume and surround yourself with, it enhances you from being postpartum. It doesn't mean you won't experience any postpartum depression but it does mean you have a better chance at fighting it and actually winning against it.

Listen to your spirit mommies and daddies. There's a reason you had a second thought to speak differently or take a different course of action.

Save yourself first 🖤

What are you feeling now that you haven't felt before?

_____

_____

_____

_____

_____

_____

_____

_____

What part of Postpartum do you feel you are experiencing?

_____

_____

_____

_____

_____

_____

_____

What do you need for this to get better for you, your baby, your friends, and your loved ones?

_____

_____

_____

_____

_____

_____

_____

_____

_____

_____

_____

_____

_____

_____

_____

_____

Day 20

Suffering in Silence ~;~Seems taboo right!?

Well, honey listen, if I could tell you all the times I've suffered and all the people I know who have suffered in silence, I would be a billionaire.

With postpartum depression being on such a widespread scale many moms and dads suffer in silence because the first sign or mention of feeling something other than happiness and love for yourself and your newborn baby people start labeling and diagnosing.

I mean let's be honest nobody really wants to be depressed let alone be depressed about having a baby. Having a baby is more than just a beautiful gift and to some it's a complete nightmare. But what happens is we tell ourselves that no one will understand, people will call me crazy, they will think I don't love my baby, I don't love myself. Then they'll be afraid to leave me alone thinking I'll hurt the baby or myself if not both of us.

The list can go on and on with what we tell ourselves during the postpartum stage. What we hardly ever tell ourselves (if we tell ourselves anything positive at all) is that we do need help, or maybe we need some space. A breath of fresh air, some time alone by ourselves, a hug, a smile, some laughter. Friends, family, counseling, a girls/guys night out. More than half of the time we don't even acknowledge that we pushed a baby out of our small portal womb. Or that we had our bodies cut open to bring life into this world.

We neglect the good and silence the suffering only to place a band aid on the hurt and pain we're experiencing to save face. I challenge any mother and father to step out of the moment you feel and open up to suffering out loud!

Speak what's ailing you and leave room for help and healing, nurturing and growth to come into you.

Shout to the world that you risked your life to create and give life!

I love you and your suffering in silence will only get louder and louder on its own if you don't learn to shout the way you prefer it to be known. Don't let your suffering speak for you.

Affirm: I chose to be a mother and my baby chose me to be it's mother. If I suffer in silence, so does my baby.

Day 21

Crying

Lawd knows I'm not a fan of hollering babies and children. Guess I got blessed to not have to deal/manage with a bunch of hollering babies my first go round as a mother. Also want to be grateful I didn't because it's a lot on it's own now and I'm an experienced mother. So imagine back then! Wooooo child thank you God/ Universe for having mercy on me. I thank my ex husband and myself for having mercy on me. One crying is enough, but two crying babies at once!? No, Thank- You At All!

Guess it's a test for me as well because DoJo feels that he needs to cry for attention. But when you give him the love and attention he's asking for he gets upset. So I'm like. "Listen man do you need to get it together or something because now you're just hollering to be hollering." If I hold you while you're crying and you still keep crying yet all of your needs are met and now all your wants, why are you crying? I wish he could talk, I know it's early but I wish he could talk. Well then keep hollering you'll get tired of hearing yourself scream while I rock you into dreamland.

Sidenote: Today we start learning more words of expression. For the life of me and in me and there's a lot of life in me and of me I could never ever understand how or why a mother would want to "silence" her baby. In all honesty I never wanted to understand. I

45

always wanted to add some patience, peace, love, and help to the ailing mother's heart and mind. So how the hell and why the hell do I have to go through this crying to understand exactly WHY they want to silence their baby? I use the word silence because no mother is thinking I'll kill my baby because he/she won't shut up. No she's thinking please stop crying, Why are you crying? I've done everything, I just want you to be happy and quiet. Because we are humans and from generation to generation we've been programmed by the things that we have experienced and seen most times we automatically resort to physical force to make people do what we want them to do. So naturally it becomes a murder when in reality all she wanted was the baby to stop crying, not die.

This is hard to write as a mother. This is hard to write as a woman. This is hard to write as a human. It's still hard even to think that at some point I too wanted my babies to be quiet. I just wanted them to stop crying. But I Am ever so very grateful I have been vulnerable and strong enough to either let them cry a little, find some type of way to soothe them and myself, Slow myself enough to handle it in the best way possible. I'm grateful I have loving, helping, teenagerrs who have been so outstanding as siblings. If it weren't for them having a breaking point with the babies crying I can honestly say I probably would've been fake toughing it out. Forcing myself into postpartum depression. My fiance is a new father and he is just getting a good swing of being a father to a son and to add a daughter I'm sure has excited and frightened him immensely. I want you all to think twice before you say you don't understand why someone says or does the things they say and do. You're not in their shoes and you definitely are not them so you don't know what you will and won't say or do until the experience becomes yours.

Know that crying is healing first and foremost mommy.

Second I want to remember and realize that babies cry ALL the time no matter what. It's how they communicate with us until they learn to talk and in some cases decide to talk. One thing that helped me was to start talking with my hands like sign language so to speak. It also helped to point out emotional faces so that my son DoJo could identify how he feels even if he cannot verbally say how he feels. It took some time and patience but I promise you it is so worth the time and patience and that little person's unwilling to give up determination. They love you and want to communicate with you in the easiest way possible. They too want to stop crying and be understood and helped and happy. Fortunately and unfortunately it is up to us as the parents to teach them how to do everything. You both are afraid and it requires patience from both of you to grow through it all together. I also learned that using actual baby sign language can help with communication as well. If technology is never good for anything it is definitely good for teaching baby sign language just by watching it consistently. If you don't want to expose the baby to technology so early like I didn't, then you watch and learn and be patient enough to teach the baby little by little.

Free Space (Draw, write, doodle, create in this space what makes you feel good, free, joy, or at peace).

DAY 21

Day 22

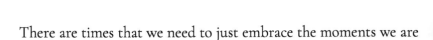

There are times that we need to just embrace the moments we are experiencing in order to get through the experience at the moment.

Sometimes the best thing is to just get through the moment and address the experience later. Not everything is meant to be learned, or addressed right away. Things take time, love takes time, healing takes time, life takes time. Time takes time lol...... My point is things happen and play out when, where, how, why, and with whomever they are meant to. You shouldn't rush things because naturally that's how we miss out on the best parts. The best lessons are learned with love, calmness, and acceptance.

What have you been having a hard time embracing or allowing yourself to experience?

_____

_____

_____

_____

_____

Space to create some positivity ...

_____

_____

_____

_____

_____

_____

_____

_____

_____

_____

_____

_____

_____

_____

_____

_____

_____

_____

Day 23

Whatever you do mommy and daddies, Stand firm within your power of self!
 Yes we're parents but we are also an individual and will remain as such

What are some things you wish you could for yourself or you would like to do for yourself?

1.

2.

3.

4.

5.

6.

7.

8.

9.

10.

I made a list of ten things and some will find this challenging while others will find this easy. For those of you who find this easy I applaud you and I thank you in advance for teaching me that putting self first isnt as hard as I make it or those like me are making it. For those of you who struggle with finding something, or anything to place on this list. Please do not under any terms or conditions blame yourself or feel bad because this is not as easy as you want it to be. Growing requires stages of pain to happen. Glowing requires shining through the darkest storms. You can choose which one of these phases you will be experiencing with this lesson. Whatever the case may be, just make sure you celebrate every little step.

What are some things you wish you had not done and what you don't want to do?

1.

2.

3.

4.

5.

6.

7.

8.

9.

10.

Now again this may be easier for others and vice versa. Celebrate your wins and every little step you take towards learning this version of you.

Day 24

Find your inner peace and happiness and never ever forget how to get back to that place!

The challenges of being a new mommy or a mommy again are very vast! However I know that as many challenges that are there are also victories and more. It's so very important to be able to smile for yourself through those tough times and challenging moments. It seems unbearable at times when a child is also struggling. The key is having your own inner peace in the middle of chaos.

This also applies to everyday life as well!

What the fuck is your own inner peace!? How can there be any inner peace when there is chaos!?

What type of shit is that and who actually achieves this!?

It's called life sister, girl, honey, child. See what a woman comes to terms with in life is that it will always be some shit going on, some shit ending, some shit just beginning. Some shit that makes sense and then there's shit that is just beyond insanity. Regardless of what type of shit it is and what it smells like or how big or small it is. The truth is one of two things will happen. Either the shit gets cleaned up or it sits there and slowly goes away on its own. Now of course there's consequences of each choice and that choice lies within your hands. The point is that you smile through whatever bullshit is in front of you, beside you, behind you, next to you, and even in you.

Some things you can do to grasp your inner peace is to first find what brings you peace. This can be listening to music, total silence, dance, art work, creativity, journaling, being with loved ones, watching a favorite show and/or reading a book, things of that nature.

Once you find what brings you peace, start implementing it into your life. Find moments of your day or time to create the space to have some inner peace. Some pieces of time to hold your inner peace and make deposits into your inner peace account. Once you have become accustomed to giving yourself some inner peace, carry your inner peace with you everyday all day.

Okay so how do you use this newfound inner peace in the middle of chaos? You breathe and know that this storm too shall pass. No matter if it rains for 40 days and 4 nights one day it has to stop and it will stop. Nothing is permanent and thighs are always shifting and changing. Sometimes you just have to acknowledge that the chaos you're experiencing isn't even you chaos to have hold onto or be consumed with. That alone will bring you inner peace because guess what, It is not your shit! Take a moment and breathe, acknowledge your five senses in the middle of the chaos. What do you see? What do you smell? What do you hear? What do you feel physically? What do you taste? Now open your eyes & smile. The storm will start to calm now.

Day 25

Each day we as mothers, fathers, parents, manage to get and grow through all that was before and teach all that is behind us.

What's done is done!

Say it with me, What's Done is DONE!

Listen I know we all have those moments of what if and if I only then things would/wouldn't be...... Well the truth is no matter what thoughts you muster up and how you psych yourself up there is absolutely nothing you can do with the past except learn from it and apply it to your NOW and your NEXT! What good is wasted time, tears, breath, mind juice, emotions and anything else for that matter on shit that has happened?

Let me ask you this......

Can you change what's ailing you about the past?

Can you fix what's ailing you about the past?

Have you ever stopped to learn the lesson in the experience from the past?

No, No, No, and uhmmmm probably another No for whatever BUT you have conjured up. SO STOP worrying about it. Stop beating yourself up because you're not helping yourself, those around, the baby/babies, or the situation. Hell you ain't even helping the lesson be received, accepted, acknowledged, or learned.

There's a time and a place for everything and every one and this time there needs to be some acceptance of serenity.

How can embracing serenity help you navigate yourself and life?

_____

_____

_____

_____

_____

_____

_____

_____

_____

_____

_____

_____

_____

_____

_____

_____

_____

Day 26

Time to eat!

I don't remember Layla, Shiya, or Jr eating so much at such a small size or age. But man oh man can

DoJo and, hell all 5 of them put some food away! Yup we learned that even little people like to eat a lot.

It makes sense because their little bodies are burning so much energy so fast.

The most valuable part of this is "PROPER nutrition is necessary in order to keep you growing and going. Now I know you think and more than likely are saying I have a good sense of nutrition for my child(children). Baby lol I Am Not speaking about your children. Only. I'm primarily speaking of you! As parents more often than not we are so focused on feeding our children that we forget that we need to feed ourselves. In all honesty most times we say, "I'll be alright as long as "they" eat, that's what matters."

This couldn't be more of a lie than the weather man talking himself. Now I'm sure you've heard the plane story before. You know if the plane is going down you save yourself first right!? Well if you haven't now you have. But that's not my story, my story of learning this lesson (and in all honesty I'm still learning to apply this lesson to my everyday all day life) is hearing my uncle tell me I need to eat in order to feed my baby because I breastfed all of my children. See I didn't realize or know that I had to take care of myself in order to take care of my baby. I was 20 when I had my first baby so obviously I was young and dumb asf when it came to truly caring for a baby. I had taken care of nieces, nephews, cousins and such but not my own. When he said that to me I immediately thought if I don't eat then I'm going to starve my baby! There was absolutely no way in hell that was going to happen. Me, starve my baby!? Absolutely fucking not! So I grabbed a piece of chicken right when he said that. Now that I've gotten older and I've learned that breastmilk is created from blood I look at things just a tad bit differently. To me no matter what you feed your body somehow, some way, it gets in your bloodstream so I'm even more careful of the things I put in my body especially because I Am currently breastfeeding. So yes I do my best to not skip meals and to make healthier eating choices. I'm not the best at putting myself first. I will admit that. What I can tell you is this. Choose not to listen to me, that's fine, but when you make that choice I want you to stop and take note how you feel about yourself and throughout your day and how you handle your day. This includes all the activities that happen in your day and more importantly how do you handle your child/children and socializing? Then I want you to just for one day put yourself first, take care of yourself first and take note of the very same things. I'll even be more honest and transparent and tell you that your first go round of putting yourself first may go horrible and you'll find yourself saying, "Shantay was wrong. I knew I should've just kept doing what I was doing and took care of me last." That's usually how it goes because guess what, "No one in your home, family, work, or life in general is used or accustomed to you putting yourself first so naturally it will and is going to ruffle the hell out of their feathers. The reward comes and it comes with you continuing to just practice putting yourself first. Even if it only starts with one thing per day until it's a natural habit/routine that everyone knows you're not happy until you have your "morning cup of coffee."

Life literally starts with YOU FIRST.

Day 27

Just let it be

Not everything nor everyone needs mommy's superhero abilities to come and save the day. Just let things be and what's meant to be saved will be saved and salvaged.

Wait what! And what is this supposed to mean to me, Shantay!? Why and how in the hell do I have a piece of mind and tend to myself but let shit just happen!?

Just like you said.

Have a sense of inner peace. Your minimum level of peace could be the maximum amount you need in whatever given moment you have the small amount of peace. Your maximum amount of peace could be the same and quite frankly it can be too much too. How I know right! Simply put you could be so zenned out you don't give a fuck what's happening as long as no one is bleeding or dying. How is this too much zen? Because typically when we say fuck it that's when we are needed and wanted and we just don't care. It's more of a balance and it's perfect for this topic because let's be honest mommy cannot solve everything and she truly shouldn't have to either. Mothers are not meant to save everyone and do everything. So please mommy stop taking everything upon yourself and making it all your responsibility to make shit shake and move and even to make ends meet. You didn't make the baby or babies by yourself so why do you have to or should you have to do it all by yourself. I know being a single mother you have to do a lot by yourself because there's no one else to turn to. But that's what sisters, cousins, brothers, aunts, uncles, friends and strangers are for. To lend a helping hand when you need it, want it, and when you don't even ask for it when you do need it, want it, and don't know who to ask or even how to begin asking for help.

The day will save itself mommy. The day will begin and finish with or without your input and most things usually work themselves out. Do what you can and are able to do without compromising your sanity, sense of self, and your ability to rise again and face the next day, challenge, or life over all.

Don't block your blessings by being so independent that everyone looks at you and thinks you got it all together.

I wanna let you know beforehand that people will not and may not do things the way you do things. So don't let that become an issue when you do decide to receive help. Don't let people half ass and be okay with things if what you think is half ass helps being their max. The part that matters is they wanted to help on their own or they agreed to help when you asked them for their help.

PS help comes in many forms, shapes, and fashions too. It isn't just one particular way to help, get help, ask for help, give help, or receive help.

Day 28

Clothes that make you look good and feel good, and some time alone to just clear your mind and let your consciousness and irritation go. Time with your bff, YOURSELF!

Have you ever had time for yourself?

_____

_____

When was the last time you took some time for yourself?

_____

_____

How did you feel when you took some time for yourself?

_____

_____

_____

_____

Are you ready to take some time for yourself?

_____

_____

What will you do with the time for yourself?

_____

_____

_____

_____

Are you afraid to be alone by yourself, with yourself?

_____

_____

_____

If you feel afraid to be alone by yourself, why do you feel afraid?

_____

_____

_____

_____

Is there someone you would like to be with you, while you have time for yourself, to yourself?

_____

_____

_____

_____

_____

_____

That sounds weird I know right? Like how do I have time for myself with myself, by myself if I have or want someone with me? Well it's not as difficult as it sounds. Sometimes a person's presence in silence has a huge impact on us. Sometimes we just want to be in silence while we have a moment to just breathe and be in whatever space we need/want to be in for that moment. There's nothing wrong with this and it's actually quite normal too. The trial is finding someone who is okay with just being present in those specific moments.

Day 29

Sisterhood!

Sis! When I tell you this time is so important during your healing!

I can't explain or say it enough. Yes there are men out there that adore pussies and women beyond belief. Yet and still!

There is nothing like having a sister circle or sisterhood no matter how near or far when it comes to vibing and healing, hell, living in general.

So please do take the time to connect with your feminine power! After all it is what got you here and what helped you get to pregnancy and postpartum in general.

I Love You Always

#WomanOfLife
#SexDoulaLoading
#BirthDoula
#SpiritualLifeCoach
#WellnessSupport

PS: Your sisterhood/sister circle can look like whatever positive environment you can conjure up that makes you feel surrounded with feminine love, power, grace, power, and assurance you need to heal and feel all that you need to feel.

Some places or websites and even apps you can use are below:

Apps:

Mindful Mamas

Yoni Circle

Facebook Groups (breast feeding, pregnancy, new moms, womb healing, woman groups) Websites:

Momni.com

Blackgirlsbreath.com

Shehealstheworld.com

Check your local community library for gatherings and your community center for women, mother, wife gatherings.

Day 30

Men have postpartum too!

I never knew this existed within a man, not to say men don't or can't understand or experience the baby blues or depression. I'm saying that I didn't know it affected men until I gave birth to DoJo. I was talking with my doula and she mentioned it to me. I was taken back a bit because all my other pregnancies and births my ex-husband appeared to be so mellow. Hell, it's probably because he smoked weed lol I'm not sure. I think the next time I talk to him I'll ask and get back with you on this. Anywho......

It affects them about the same and in different ways as well. I've been researching it to find out as much as possible. Right now check in on your child's father. He may need some help in some type of way.

Here are some ways new fathers and first time fathers experiencing postpartum:

Not having male guidance or loss of their own father. Not having their father around through or during their upbringing, so they feel like they are incapable of being a father.

Fear, resentment, lacking financially, pride, ego, comparing themselves to other fathers or ideas of what they think a father should or shouldn't be. Feeling like they haven't achieved the recognition to be a father which could be self doubt. Traumatic birth experiences with the mother of their baby(ies), miscarriages, disabled children, feeling inadequate like they won't be a good father now that they are a father, failure before they even fail, emotionally unavailable, Over all just not knowing how to be a father.

Things you can do to help them is just be there. I've learned that most times they just want someone to be there and be present while they grow through things on their own in their own time. On the other hand there are men who want you involved with talking and working, growing through things together. Personally I feel like this is the absolute best! At least you both know you are NOT alone in the postpartum stage or parenting or being an adult and actually allowing yourself to be human and have fears and emotions.

At the very least if there is nothing that helps please seek help and the best place to start seeking help is your postpartum check up. I know it's something new, however you mom and dad are able to receive postpartum help through your Midwife, Nurse Practitioner, OB GYN, or PCP by simply answering the questionnaire. Also please note you can bring postpartum concerns to the people listed above for at least the first year of your baby/babies life after birth.

Please know that you do not and you should not face any signs of postpartum alone. There are many forms of postpartum so don't feel like just because you love your baby tht postpartum is not or has not affected you in some way. The spectrum of postpartum is very vast so don't single yourself out.

Be honest with yourself and have the conversation
open heartedly.

Day 31

Alright enough is enough!

Yeah it's only so long before a mother will stop accepting a dirty ass house. Yes, being in an unclean or an uncomfortable environment can be a part of depression and postpartum depression too.

If I have to stay inside, at least let it be nice and clean. Let me have a sense of purity within these four walls to enhance my moments of peace.

They say cleanliness is next to godliness and women are the only ones that can create life like god.

Don't lower, or diminish a woman's energy, power, or vibration by allowing dirt or dust to settle.

One sense of cleanliness at a time.

By that I mean start by straightening up. Then take it one room at a time or one task at a time. Don't just jump back into being the maid as though your womb is not still wide, the hell open due to a whole small human being coming out of you. Your bones aren't even in the right positions again.

If you do nothing but separate the laundry then that's a start and guess what someone hopefully will recognize that you are sorting the laundry and may begin the process to get the laundry done. Put the dishes in the dish rack up and then hopefully someone else can wash the dishes. Vacuum and someone else can dust. Sweep and someone else can mop, you get the picture by now hopefully.

My ultimate favorite is to make sure my bed is made and things are picked up off the floor and placed in their proper places. Don't forget to open the blinds/curtains and spray some non toxic air freshener, light a natural candle, burn an incense, use some essential oils in your diffusers or air purifiers. Sage! If the weather permits, open a window or more, let some fresh air in.

Make your home or space as comfortable as possible piece by peace.

Take a moment and jot down some things you can do for your level of comfort and sanity to increase ...

_____

_____

_____

_____

_____

_____

_____

_____

_____

_____

_____

_____

Day 32

Sometimes you just have to let the babies be babies!

Yes, we're meant to nurture love, care for, and more. But what we aren't told is to let the babies be babies as much as we should be telling that to ourselves.

Trust me it takes the stress away of expecting the baby to listen and understand you. It gives you the opportunity to just breathe and know that it won't stay the way it is always.

What does this mean? How do you let a baby be a baby?

Babies get dirty, babies don't listen, they just wanna play, laugh, love, eat, sleep, drink all of whatever is in your cup, and have fun. Babies have bad days just like adults and other children do. Sometimes that could mean they wanna be left alone. Sometimes they wanna cuddle and be loving. Sometimes you just have to let the baby be themselves and choose to fight the battle of teaching another day. Every day does not have to be so serious and perfect.

I know you've seen a mother with a child that has on rain boots, a hoodie and some pajama pants or shirt. Hell, you've probably seen a child with a Halloween costume on and wondered exactly what the hell or why the hell the mother chose to let them come out of the house the way they did. The truth is some days just flow a lot smoother when you just allow them to have their days and moments just like you wished others would allow you to have your days and moments.

I promise you it's less stressful when you allow this to just be sometimes. You feel better and so do they. The best part is you get to see their little imaginations grow and blossom.

There's a reason why they wanna wear the weird looking ensemble they have put together. Some things happening in their mind trust and believe.

Day 33

Sometimes you have to let the ends of life connect in order for you to find your middle ground.

Sometimes it all seems impossible but all that means is you need to remind yourself that you are possible, it is possible, look in the mirror and say, "I'm possible."

You got this mommy

The silver lining of life is simply knowing that everything has an ending and a beginning. Being in the middle of that and holding your peace in that space is so detrimental to you just learning to groove and flow with life. Earlier I said we shouldn't have to make ends meet, at least not by ourselves. However sometimes the unfortunate truth is we do have to make ends meet and making ends meet sometimes means standing in the middle and finding or figuring out exactly where each end is in order for them to meet. One end can be good and the other can be bad. Sometimes they're both good/bad. Either way the ends ust connect to become a full circle.

Sometimes being a mom or new mom, and first time mom means that we don't' feel as though we can handle the crying, the shouting, the temper tantrums, always being a mommy. Hell sometimes we just wanna walk the fuck away and never return. Now some of us are able to do just that, walk away and never return while others walk away momentarily. For those who are strong and vulnerable enough to walk away and never return, I tip my hat to you because although my children can and know how to work every nerve I have and don't know I have, I can't imagine myself not ever being in their lives again. I think a mother who is honest enough to say, "I'm not the mother for them," or "My child deserves more than what I can give", is beyond powerful and they deserve recognition for choosing better. Now I'm not saying that the mother shouldn't give mothering her best shot. I'm not even saying this is always best for the child/children because sometimes this proves to be the worst outcome for the child/children. What I Am saying is as a mother and a woman, a sister, a niece, an aunt, an ex wife, and human being. We have to stop pushing ourselves beyond known limits. Stop pushing ourselves beyond a boundary we know we will only be so good at. We all have a max and we have to be okay with our own max in order for others to be okay with it. Accepting our own maximum limits allows others to accept us for who we are and how we want and deserve to be received.

Give and receive yourself with the same amount of love you give and receive others with and the way you want to be received and loved. That's the best way to make ends meet and it's also the best way for you to see just how possible you truly are and how impossib;e life would be without you in your child/children's lives.

Write your first Affirmation of how possible you are and your second one of how possible you want to be received. Tear the bottom of this paper off and place it where you can see it daily, you'll need it and be happy you did it.

_____

_____

_____

_____

_____

_____

_____

_____

_____

_____

_____

_____

_____

_____

Day 34

Give yourself a break and if you have to, start fresh again.

All too often being a mommy means things change all the time!

My, my, my, how frustrating that can be! Aaaahhhhh dammit I know because when things change that means mommy has to toughen up, suck it up, get it together, and help everyone else with the change.

That isn't always easy because well, not everyone handles change the same.

The beauty of this all is you get to willingly leave a lot of things in the past!

I mean we are starting over if necessary right!?

Happy New Decade Mommy 2020

This is where it all began and where it all ended for all of us.

Change can be the worst and it can seem like the worst. We don't view change as a good thing enough to embrace change as actually being good. Even when change is bad it still is good because again good things and bad things come to an end. Everyone's lives began changing on this very day. We had no idea what was upon us and some of us intuitively knew something catastrophic was about to take place. What we didn't know is that the way of life would be and could be changed forever as far as we know.

Rewind<<

This year is going to be one of my greatest years! It's my life path number 4, our life path number 4. I just gave birth to my 5th child, I'm engaged to finally be married. I'm focused solely on my business financially and although the year didn't end the way I would have preferred for it to end. It ended and here's the opportunity for me, for us to start fresh, to start new, the beginning of a new decade. A whole new world, a whole new cycle of life. How swiftly things change, within the first 10 days of starting a new 10 years of life. I learned what was missing in my own life and that was me. I was so worried and distraught, traumatized from others leaving me that I actually left myself. I left myself out there in the cold for someone else to save me and heal me. I left myself out there in the wide open spaces of life without a shield of protection seeking loyalty and protection, seeking to be cherished and valued as a mother. An open wound/womb to be nurtured and cared for by someone other than myself.

This is where I drew the line in the sand

This is where I dared any fucking body to cross that line, it was either you or me and at this moment I chose and promised myself and my children, my future, that it would never ever be Shantay ever again.

I was afraid and I felt all alone. I felt like if I Am to be afraid and feel alone then I can and will do damn fucking good on my own.

Day 35

Have a little faith in yourself!

With everything we face in life we find the strength and the courage, the optimism to do and be, the faith to believe and encourage everyone except for self.

Somebody tell me who the fuck said we should choose others over self!?

Why is this even a thing?

What sane self loving, unconditional self loving person thought it was right or it made sense to have faith in something else and someone else without first having faith in self?

I don't know what dummy summoned this demon or bad entity because it most definitely is a force to be reckoned with. But I smite thee!

YES I SMITE THEE!

In my mind, my eyes, and my now experience would postpartum even be a thing if we were taught to first love and believe in ourselves? I personally think not. I think not because if we love and believe in ourselves and we had just a smidget of faith in self then what we water grows. Clearly we all water having faith in other things and people because that's what grows faster than faith in self.

Well with the new year here I challenge you to make your new year resolution having faith in you, believing in you, watering you like you have done for so many other things and people.

A little faith in self every day helps make the negativity go further and further away. It disrupts the constant negative self talk and thoughts. It diminishes the bad emotions and it does away with self let downs. Having faith in yourself helps you know that at the very least you gave your all and did all that you could do, were capable and able to do, and all you were meant to do.

When you have faith in yourself, others have faith in you too.

What's an area of faith you can devote to yourself and how can you start devoting that faith?

_____

_____

_____

_____

_____

_____

_____

_____

_____

_____

Day 36

Trust yourself through this and anything else you saw yourself accomplishing for you and your babies/family.

Mommies are more than superheroes

On a daily basis we do so much in such a small amount of time and space to say the least. There's little to no help and sometimes there is an abundance of help. But in all honesty not many if any can or will do it like mommy does it. The truth is no one should be able to trump mommy and her love, care, dedication, and anything else that comes from her, of her. We are the life bringers and the same energy is a force to be reckoned with as well. Lately I've been saying I'm just a mom. Truth be told, I Am just a Mom. But I'm more than just a mom. I'm more than a damn good mom, I'm more than the superhero my children actually look up to. I'm every single thing and being their little big hearts desire. Even when they desire other people, places, and things. I know, I Know, just a little while ago I said we don't have to be superheroes and we aren't. However with all that we do even a superhero can't keep up with us! We are beyond the superheroes, we are more like the alien life.

Laugh and bust your gut laughing if you must. The truth is who in the hell on this earth could, or has actually been able to keep up with real live mothers?

I know, no one!

So I dare to take a moment and pick a cape, burn a cape or whatever you choose to do but whatever you choose to do please know and receive that you birth superheroes, Superheroes do not birth or compare to you Dear Momma!

What is it or what all do you do that you know is beyond superhero ability or capability?

Go Crazy With This List Because WE Deserve It!

1.

2.

3.

4.

5.

6.

7.

8.

9.

10.

11.

12.

Day 37

*Find some time to create the joy
your soul desires*

It's already inside of you, you have to allow yourself to set it free.
Fly like a bird
If you aren't artsy or crafty, do the following:

- Get you a poster board
- Print out some pictures
- Cut out some pictures from magazines or whatever/ wherever you find pictures you like
- Get you a good glue stick
- Get some glitter
- Get border paper
- Get a journal/notebook that the cover art resonates within you
- Pick out some cute pens/markers/color pencils
- Take some pictures with your phone/camera and create a folder called "My Joy"
- Get a map of the world

- Some thumbtacks or stick pins
- Get a cork board/white board

The point is to create a space or piece of the people, places, and things that bring you joy so you can start taking the initiative to bring yourself some joy by fulfilling this visual crafty bucket list of joy. You see we mothers can dream up a lot of things and we can make a lot of shit happen

Day 38

One day you will wish they were still tiny just like right now you wish they were big lol Talk about balance lmao 😄🫦

As I reflect on these moments of when my teenagers were tiny, and even with my current two little ones I still have that "awwww my baby is growing up!" I even have those I wish he/she was still an infant even with the crying that can and does kind of drive me insane from time to time. I feel like when they're tiny it's so enjoyable because of the loving and the cuddling and the baby smell!

Oh My Goodness, the new baby scent is soooooo yummy and captivating. It's one you don't want to ever let go of. Fresh, new baby scent is so loving, peaceful, and full of joy! I'm a mother of five and I promise you I have always wondered what smells so good inside my womb that makes my babies smell so damn good. I just love to sniff them lol. But that is not the only reason you want them to stay tiny or be tiny. It's so many other reasons that we want them to stay tiny and be tiny again.

If you never felt good about being a mother or father or parents, if you're doing this together then take a moment to sit down as a parent/parents and jot the joys you have witnessed and felt being a mother/father to such an amazing bundle of joy. Remember you only get one shot at this with each and every individual baby you will ever bring into this realm. These moments are yours for keeping and cherishing. They are here and are meant for you to hold onto and to build that long lasting love bond as parent and child with your baby no matter what age they are and what age you are they will ALWAYS be your baby and you will always see them as "Your Baby" still doing the same ole baby things that they do as an actual baby.

1.

2.

3.

4.

5.

6.

7.

8.

9.

10.

11.

12.

13.

14.

15.

16.

17.

18.

19.

20.

21.

Day 39

One of the best things you can give a mother is some time by herself for a peaceful hot flipping shower or bubble bath!

AND DON'T WAKE UP THE BABY (BABIES)!

That is it and that is all!

I HAVE said my peace I SAID WHAT I SAID

PS

Mommies do NOT be afraid to let this be known otherwise you'll be ready to rip someone's head off just for 15-20 minutes or time by yourself to cleanse yourself.

Cleanliness is next to Godliness and no matter how you slice it WOMEN and only WOMEN are able to create life like God can create life sooooo with no further adieu......PLEASE ALLOW YOUR GodIs to have a moment to cleanse

A happy clean mother is one of the best mommys you could ever have

When a woman/mommy feels clean she feels happy and free for lack of better words.

She feels fresh like that brand new baby!

It helps get rid of stress.

It soothes and heals.

It replenishes her on multiple levels.

It nurtures her!

Mommy it is imperative that you care for yourself with cleanliness. A good hot shower or bath (using intimate and delicate products) can help you in a lot of ways. Don't ever succumb to always taking quick showers, not bathing at all, and more importantly washing baby with you ALL-THE-TIME! There are products out there curated specifically for postpartum nurturing and healing. Some of the products I have used and still use are below. You can choose from what I've listed or do your own research. The point is to use your intuition, listen and be obedient to what your mind, body, spirit, and vagina is asking for.

Yoni Wash-by the Goddess Box

Nourish Me Creations- has postpartum tea and herbal mixes for postpartum healing. She also has waist beads that are created intuitively for healing as well. Ask about her vaginal pads for postpartum too.

Peaceful Birthing Doula-has body butter for healing your skin after your bath, so you don't have that saggy wrinkly skin.

You can put your own herbal mixes together based on what you know your body needs and wants. There's also yoni oils out there as well. I'm looking into these myself and I'm very picky about what I do when it comes to my healing and my vagina.

You can use this space to jot down some notes and ideas that come to mind because I know your womb and your mind body and spirit are speaking as you read so feel free to get to healing sis. This isn't just about the baby or babies. It's about you because babies wouldn't be here if it wasn't for our wombs ●

Day 40

When it all seems so right something always decides to go wrong. Or is it wrong because it doesn't fall in line with the rest of things? Whatever it is, trust that it all is happening according to your plan. The plan to get you where you are going.

Your destiny. Don't give up now mommy

I'm sick of this shit in all honesty! One day I'm happy the next moment I'm sad or angry, and the problem is I don't know why any of this is happening besides my fucking hormones being out of whack! I just gave birth to two babies back to back, I lost my job in my career path because I was pumping at work. I'm always home alone with the babies. These babies cry A LOT! I'm not used to crying babies! I'm not even used to this damn roller coaster of emotions after birth.

At some point I had to sit down and be honest with myself. More so accept the truth that is in front of me and all around me. This shit is not how I saw it being. For the record, no sis I didn't dream of a fairytale. I trusted him and myself, I trusted us and the process of love growing because love takes time. It definitely takes even more time when you're healing. I just don't wanna be home alone with babies by myself all the time. I don't wanna be in a relationship but be a single mother. I don't wanna be figuring this shit out by my damn self all the time. I don't want him chiming in only when he feels like it or because something doesn't sit well with him based on how I'm mothering or being a woman and healing. I don't wanna put in all the work of raising the babies to the point of walking and talking and then here his ass comes being daddy now because it isn't as tedious when babies can't walk or talk.

Where the fuck are you when I not just need you but when I want you and deserve you because that's what you said you want and that's what you said you will do! You're NOT FUCKING HERE and you haven't been! Where are you? We need you, we want you here, with US! Who are you? They don't know you, they deserve to know you, they came here as yours because they want to know and they chose to be your babies. I know money has to be made to take care of a family but there's millions of ways to make millions of dollars. Brothers, fellas, men, fathers, and baby daddies...... don't be super daddy when your baby starts walking and talking. WE, meaning mother and baby or babies need and want you to be super daddy from the moment we (meaning you and me) get pregnant. You're not alone sis at some point we've all experienced being alone with babies and wanting the father to be there through it all. Some of us get blessed for things to make a turn for the best and then there are those of us who have to continue on without the father or with the father being part time. Whatever your case may be, know that there IS a man or men out there willing to help you and you don't have to fuck or be in a relationship with them either. There's friends, family and communities of sisterhood and brotherhood. YOU unfortunately have to reach out and be vulnerable to say you need/want help, ask for it and then allow the help to be given.

It takes time and openness to receive.

I Love You Always

Day 41

Altered moments create blessed memories!

So yeah what you contemplated on doing didn't happen because it wasn't meant to happen.

What's meant to happen will always happen whether you want to participate in it or not.

Just know your position and fulfill it to the best of your ability.

What do I mean by this?

Well we don't always get to control the events of life let alone our day to day living. So when circumstances and situations challenge us in ways we cannot control what is happening or about to happen, even when we can't control the outcome. We must just embrace the moment and take away everything that transpired. You can sort through it all later. The goal is to eventually take the best pieces of these types of moments and happenings and go forth.

As women, mothers, and people over all please stop allowing yourself and your life to be consumed by the uncontrollable things that happen. We have to stop attempting to control what is not meant to be controlled. WE must learn to accept that we have to trust the world, the universe, God, the cycles, the process and sometimes all of that includes some pain and trying times.

Sit with yourself and write down some things that were not in your control but they worked themselves out and you are now able to let go of the bad memories and embrace the lessons you learned.

_____

_____

_____

_____

_____

_____

_____

_____

_____

_____

_____

_____

_____

_____

_____

_____

Now that you have some clarity that you've made it through, you've grown through the uncontrollable things in life. Make a plan of action to be mindful enough to position yourself to grow and glow through the times that will happen in your life.

_____

_____

_____

_____

_____

_____

_____

_____

_____

_____

_____

_____

_____

_____

_____

_____

_____

Day 42

The more womb and spiritual healing I do the more protective I become over myself. In the words of Iya, my yoni egg Empress...... Guard the Pu$$y Gates!

Listen, WE as women allow people, places and things in our lives, our, mind, body, soul, spirit, and into our worlds, universe, wombs, and heart! It is up to US to choose wisely! It is up to US to use our intuition and discernment to make OUR own World a better place to live, thrive, and dwell in. We can't always blame others for Who, What, and Where we allow inside of US. The more connected you become to your world, your womb the more protective you are and the more aware and mindful you are with making decisions and more importantly the better you are at listening to yourself, your spirit, your guides, your ancestors, God, or whatever higher power you follow. In this case it truly should be yourself!

Here are some ways you can become more accustomed to your Womb and the wounds it holds to heal them and to better protect her, him, and you.

- Spiritual baths
- Self pleasure
- Intentional hygiene care
- Using specific products (preferably non toxic and/or organic) that syncs with your body chemistry

- Meditations to tune into yourself, what is it that pushes you to be so disconnected from your womb, yourself, and your inner world?

- Journaling what is going on inside so you are able to see yourself on the outside

- Yoni egg, yoni pearls, yoni steams, and yoni teas

- Sexual healing (take precautions with this because you can heal yourself before looking and wanting others or someone else to heal you. Yes your male partner has the ability to heal you but know that if he is not in alignment with himself then you could very well deplete him while he is healing you. YOu don't want that because then you have to heal him and then there is this constant cycle of healing each other versus healing and then growing and glowing together).

- Affirmations, mirror magick,

- EXERCISE & FOOD, these help your body flow and move, what you put in must come out. So please be mindful of how you treat your body physically and what you consume. Toxic foods and products create more dis-ease. More things you have to figure out in order to reach your fulfilled destiny. ~Obedience, Obedience, Obedience. Your body and yes your womb will ask for exactly what it needs to thrive and live joyfully. It is your responsibility to actually listen and actively listen at that. Believe in yourself that you can and will attain your goal.

Day 43

If you never believe anything or anyone please believe that you are the best mother you are capable of being in this moment.

Each moment we are required or we are being summoned to be a different mommy for different children, different moments, situations, purposes, and emotions.

Never doubt your ability to mother you were built and created to be the mother you are being.

If somehow you feel as though it isn't enough then be the mommy you wish you had and still would like to have.

#WomanOfLife

#MyChildrensBestMommy

#MotherOf5

Write down the things or parenting practices that you wish you had with or from your parents. DO 10 things from your mother and 10 things from your father. This will help in creating a balance in parenting with you and your child's father. It will also help with the things you are seeking from your other half as a father and parenting partner.

1.

2.

3.

4.

5.

6.

7.

8.

9.

10.

11.

12.

13.

14.

15.

16.

17.

18.

19.

20.

Day 44

Stop ●

I know it can get hard and it seems like there's no one there and the help is the bare minimum to none.

I just want you to stop and leave things be. But more importantly stop and allow people to love you and help you!

Allow People To Love You

As easy as this sounds it can be very hard to do. You see love is just a word but it's also a verb it shows action!

Love is taking you out for breakfast

Love is opening the doors for you

Love is tending to the babies for you

Love is listening to you talk and having a conversation with you

Love is holding your hand just because

Love is a passionate kiss because you deserve it and you're irresistible after birth

Love is you and you are love.

Yes it gets hard and we all want to reject love when love and life gets hard. But that's the time we need to and should be embracing love and life the most!

Kiss 🌀 it better

Day 46

Organized Where!?

Oh the beauty and joy organization holds!

But when you have a one year old running around tearing up everything you cleaned up and a one month old screaming every time you put her down. Being organized is the first and last thing on your mind.

First because, well, hell, you need to know where the hell everything is! Last because sometimes it just can't be the way you want it and you have to roll with the dice 🎲.

I want things to be so much more than what they are. But I'm grateful they are as good as they are because shit could be WAY WORSE than it is now.

In due time things will be better than they are and even more up to my personal expectations.

That doesn't and does include the babies because they are constantly growing. So that means they are constantly changing but also set in their own personality as well.

Take things for what they are and know that it isn't permanent. Life changes, people change, cycles change, everything changes even energy and what seems permanent.

Day 47

WHAT!? *It's only been 46 days!?*

It seems like it's been longer than that and it seems like I'm stronger than I really am. Like I'm ready and I'm not, like I got this and I don't!

Ugh FUCK! 😤💀

Yup that's parenting/mothering.

It's like shit never has a gray area. It's either good or bad very rarely is it ever not so bad as it seems. Even when it is, it still leans more to one side than the other. Sometimes we just want everything to be smooth sailing ⛵ and happy ☺. That's a mother's dream come true. But it wouldn't be worth the time and effort if we had nothing to push us to WANT & NEED these moments.

Let a sigh of relief happen mommy this too shall pass. Even though things seem different than they really are, know that you are operating at your best in this moment. Things become better and greater when you become better and greater.

That doesn't mean it's all on your shoulders or it's all your responsibility. But it does mean that YOU, MOMMY, must find your inner peace and balance in order to sync with nature, life, and all things moving and flowing. #EnergyHealth

Day 48

One thing I know every mother goes through is wishing she would have made a better decision. Hoping she makes the right decision, and even more knowing she has done a great job nurturing and raising her child/children.

Being the best mother/mom she is able to be.

Let me assure you sis! It gets frustrating, irritating, you have outstanding days and you have days from hell. but that's just it, it is just another day.

Another day that you conquered, be it with someone, or alone, "You Conquered It!"

Yes we make bad decisions, we make bad choices, we have bad judgment, we wish we could change things and so much more. What I want you to know is as long as you know and truly did your best then don't beat yourself down. We learn from what didn't go right and what wasn't right. It's life that's for damn sure.

Now unless you were out there acting all willie nillie don't hold it against yourself. I know our children are what really matters but if you did your best then they saw you do your best and they don't think ill of you knowing you gave it your all and what was right for the moment and situation.

Day 49

To me the worst thing a mother can say or feel is that she doesn't want to be a mother anymore. When I tell you the pressures of life and being a mother have the ability to send you into that mindset, It more than not has the ability to send you into that mindset.

Postpartum depression can play a huge role in this and have you resent being a mother, hell it will have you resent being a woman and embracing love and so much more. It will make you welcome death!

I know being in this mindset can make you feel all the feels, but I encourage you to not get wrapped up in those thoughts and feelings. They don't lead you into anything good. Don't allow yourself to get lost in such a low vibration it sounds so hard and so simple at the same time. All it takes is the sound of a different vibration and the will power to release and let go.

What are some things you can do to get yourself out of a low vibrational energy, spirit, mindset?

1.

2.

3.

4.

5.

6.

7.

8.

9.

10.

11.

12.

13.

14.

15.

16.

Day 50

Resentment!

Sis listen don't feel bad for ever feeling what you feel! Yes, that includes feeling resentment. See it's a natural thing to feel like "damn I shouldn't have had a baby/babies." How is it natural?

Uhm before you got pregnant 🧍 you were YOU! Yeah sure you carried and nurtured that little person inside of YOU. But that's it! You were still just YOU prior to conception. Then here comes pregnancy, labor, and birth and now just like that you have this little wiggling, crying, loving person depending solely on YOU!

It's like overnight you aren't just YOU anymore! Like wtf happened? At first it's all joy and excitement and then you're like noooooo take it back! 👶♀

It's more than okay sis, as long as you aren't stuck in feeling resentment! It comes and goes but don't allow it to stay forever.

Get up, get out, do something just for YOU. Because after all you are still you even though someone so precious depends on YOU!

You still depend on YOU.

Who were you prior to pregnancy?

Who did you become when you got pregnant?

Who were you after birthing a new life?

Who are you Now?

Who are you aspiring to become?

Day 51

Celebrate Birth!

It's about damn time we stop focusing on what all could be better and what will never get better.

Birth!

Birth is beautiful even in its ⊠painful, traumatic, unforgettable experience. Yes it has the ability to be bad, trust me I get it! I gave birth to 5 children all natural. I have my share of birth stories. But after all of the emotional ups and downs through labor and birth you brought home the best gift a mother could ever get! Her baby!

It was more than worth it all. Celebrate your baby, your children over all.

It's an experience like no other and each baby gave/gives you a different experience throughout labor into birth, becoming a mother, and a new woman.

You did it sis no matter how you wanted it to happen, it happened and YOU DID IT!

What did you envision your birth story being?

_____

_____

_____

_____

_____

_____

What did your birth story actually turn out to be and how has or did that affect you, your partner, the family?

_____

_____

_____

_____

_____

_____

_____

_____

_____

Day 52

Ughhh super emotional 😭 right now!

Counseling and a 6wk postpartum check all in one day right behind each other.

I wish there was a sister circle around me I could just go hide in and heal like I'm supposed to. Feeling alone and abandoned after giving birth... ...Is that shit even normal!? Some will say yes and others will beg to differ in opinions, and experience. You have to understand that people feel on the same levels; it's the experience that is not the same. Meaning some women feel abandoned and alone because everyone has shifted their attention from her (being pregnant the focus is primarily on the woman and sometimes on the baby more) to the baby. Then there are times that a woman will feel abandoned in general because she is literally left alone and abandoned. It's hard to say what is and isn't normal, what matters is and what the truth holds is that in some form shape or fashion you as a woman and now mother have felt alone and abandoned. How do we fix that? How do we face that and feel that so we can allow ourselves to let go of the pain? The answers vary because each woman's experience varies. For me it's having sisters, sistars. What I've learned is that all of your girls ain't gone speak to you the same way or in the same tone/context. The connection is different but the amount of love is the same equally. Each sister gives you something different. Something that you need inside of you to feel that wholeness and completeness as a woman and mother. A sister, a friend, a wife, niece, aunt, teacher, nurturer and so on, so forth. These types of circles are created based off love and the empathy to heal not just self but each other. Find your connect and link arms until your life and those lives with your are 360 degrees Full Moon Circle ~;~

#SearchingForOne

To Be Continued

Day 53

Man so many emotions come with being a woman, being pregnant, birthing a baby, being in a relationship, being a woman, being a boss, being a woman lol You get my point!

But what I really want you to focus on is finding the time and "making the time" to release those emotions in a healthy manner as a woman. Yesterday my mind, body, and spirit was everywhere except where it truly needed and wanted to be. So after I took care of business with my own counseling, and 6 wk postpartum check. I stopped to take time for my spirit and my heart, so my mind could sync with the two and I could sleep better and smile genuinely.

It wasn't easy!

There was a moment I wanted to cry and held back the tears because I was in public in front of people.

There was a time I didn't want to cry because I felt like it was a waste of time.

There was a time I made room to cry and I couldn't anymore.

There came the time that my tears flowed like they had been fighting to do for so long!

I was angry, hurt, confused, not sure of myself, and more importantly I just wanted to be alone! I wanted to stop and let go of everything just to have me for myself, by myself, with myself! I'm tired of sharing ME!

Then I started taking pictures, I started writing, I started listening to music, I couldn't write anymore, I could only sit there looking and listening as I cried. I realized that it was so much happiness, releasing and growth around me that I needed to embrace it! I needed to embrace me! I did that by enjoying the comfort within my spirit and the peace within each tear that fell from my eyes. Now I'm ready, I'm ready to smile again, I'm ready to go about myself again, I'm ready to go about my life again. I'm ready to allow the sun to set on everything that held me back and everyone that held me hostage.

Taking in the brisk air and the scenery around me I felt a tiny seed become planted within me, it was like a sigh of release to move on. Tiny enough it's hard for the eye to see but enough for water to touch and make it grow.

What are you nurturing inside of you for yourself? Could it be self love, confidence, compassion, or peace? What needs that motherly love and care inside of you?

_____

_____

_____

_____

_____

_____

_____

_____

Day 54

Why in the hell did I have more children? Why did I have children at all 🐼 ?

They do all the things I don't like and then they do all the things that fill my life, my mind, my body, my spirit with emotions I can't even describe.

Why in the "WOULDN'T" I have children?

Guess what, it doesn't mean you love your children any less because you question the decisions you made in the past. Children will be children and guess what? When they grow up the cycle only repeats itself. Don't nail yourself to the coffin, parenting can, will and should be challenging.

Now write down all the good things you do as a mother/mom

_____

_____

_____

_____

_____

_____

_____

Then write down the things "YOU" think are bad that you do as a mother/mom Resolve the bad list in one of two ways:

_____

_____

_____

_____

_____

_____

_____

_____

_____

Acknowledge what's on the list and let it go. Either it's a big deal or it ain't. If it ain't that much of a big deal then you can burn it, shred it, bury it, hide it, do whatever you feel is letting it go but be okay with what's on the paper and let it go.

Take the bad list as a plan of action, A To-Do List, A progress list, something that means you're working on creating a change. Create an action plan, prioritize the list, make goals for achieving things, cheer yourself on, celebrate your wins and your losses only if you put your best foot forward.

Day 55

For the RECORD, I DO NOT LIKE BREAST FEEDING DURING GROWTH SPURTS SAM I AM!

Two days up nursing this little hungry girl and comfort nursing too. So it was literally non stop!

Get off of me please!

I know, I KNOWWWWW one day I'll be wishing she would at least hug me again. So even though I wanted her off of me for my sanity and her emotional energy balance, I did embrace the moments. We slept on the couch together when we did get a chance to sleep. Otherwise we were laughing and smiling at each other and she would giggle, yes giggle at such a small age.

Nursing through a growth spurt requires patients and inner peace. Let me tell you I was at my wits end yesterday morning and then I remembered I have these magickal woosah capsules in a bottle. Talk about help and miracles getting through. I was saved, that's for sure. It isn't like making a bottle and then once the bottle is empty the baby is fine for a moment after they burp and then repeat.

It was on constantly!

Nursing to eat, Nursing to comfort, nursing because she doesn't like or want a pacifier. Nursing because she cried, nursing because my boob got close to her face, nursing, nursing,

NURSINGGGGGG lol I was done and didn't feel like there was anything left in me to give to her.

To top it all off she was spitting up from time to time. So that made me not want to give her anymore.

But we got through it all.

What I would suggest for the other mommies out there.

Have extra milk on hand so the baby isn't always on you for all of these reasons less and more. And if your baby is anything like my little mermaid. Then meditate, breathe, pray, cry, smile, laugh, be happy, be tired, Be You and know that it will end, temporarily but it will end.

Happy Friday Y'all!

Day 56

Take a nap sis

Turn on some sleep music, turn off the lights, close the blind, quiet the house, light a candle, turn on some string lights, burn some essential oils, rib some on you, turn on an air diffuser, do whatever and all that you need and want to do to take the best damn nap you can imagine.

Rest Well & Sweet Dreams

Day 57

Exercise!

It helps move your energy and your emotions. Oh and might I say it makes you fine as hell too sis!

Hopefully you have had your postpartum check up. Hopefully you have clearance to move around and stay healthy and strong. Exercise, balances hormones, helps and maintains blood flow, emotions, and clears your mental capacity. It helps you think, feel, and express yourself with a more clear state of mind. It also helps you look good as hell too. P90X is one of my favorite yoga exercise routines, outdoor walks/runs, bike riding, and being in the water because I can't swim. If there is someone out there willing to teach me please by all means help me because I would love to learn how to swim. There are apps, tv, youtube, facebook and more that can and will provide you with things to do even with you just having a baby/babies. There are mom groups that specialize solely in postpartum exercise.

Jot down some sites you've viewed for exercise, or areas of focus you would like to add some tender love and care to.

_____

_____

Two weeks worth with two days off for rest days

1.

2.

3.

4.

5.

6.

7.

8.

9.

10.

11.

12.

Goal:

_____

Completed Within:

_____

Reward:

_____

Day 58

Silence is truly Golden

A quiet woman has more power than one who always has something to say. There is more than just energy in your words. There's life death and power within your entire vibrating being

Hold Your Power

Own Your Power

Be Your Power

You Are Power

Day 59

It's the little things that matter the most!

It's as simple as hey girl! I Love You Always and I mean it

XoXo

Day 60

••*I quit! I give up! I'm finished!*

I'm not cut out for this anymore.

Sometimes that's what parenting feels like, no matter what age the children are. Can we give up? Sure some of us can. Should we give up?

Yup some of us should. There's always someone out there to pick up where we left off. I'm not telling you to give up, I'm telling you to know your limit as a parent.

Every single parent on this planet needs help. Some of us just need to let go and allow someone else more capable to step in. It doesn't mean you failed, it means you gave your child your best shot. Who knows, a breather helps us all collect ourselves whether we believe it or not.

You'll be more than okay mommy. I know how tough it can seem and how tough it actually is sometimes.

I love you and I know you always do your best.

Day 61

Discipline

Yup, you and the babies have to come to common ground and get some discipline in order so you can flourish mommy!

Take a deep breath and start working through it while implementing discipline as needed and necessary. It will be a little hurtful at first but trust me when I tell you the weight on your shoulders changes.

You have to start your children in the right direction and keep them in the right direction for them to know, see, and do the right things. That way when the wrong things and people do present themselves they know this is not the best and will not be what's for their best interest. Discipline does not mean whooping your child. It can simply mean saying no. Put them on a schedule, Not letting them have juice all day every day. Teaching and enforcing manners when they can talk. Hell potty training is discipline and a lot of mothers want that without putting in the work. People think potty training is so much better than a diaper when the truth is no honey it is not!

Do you have a bathroom in your back pocket? I think not. So what you may think it means is really a healthy lesson for your child/ children. Let's not forget to shed light on how it takes weight off of your shoulders. Some folks call it a schedule, a routine. Having order in your home or a good sense of structure, and upbringing. I call it home training for life.

❀

Day 62

At some point you learn to tune out the crying as long as it isn't a screeching, agony, pain type of crying.

Yup I'm sick of it lmao. Don't sit here and act like you ain't over this shit. All this damn crying for no reason. I feel like Bernie Mack talk, yell, scream, holla do something besides cry. Shit!

Wave your arms, shake your head yes or no lol help me out, do something babies.

Cry. Cry, and cry some more. Cry louder, and longer. Cry and then just randomly stop. Cry while I hold you, Cry when I put you down, Just sit here or lay right here and cry.

Hell cry with the baby/babies mommy. Cry together just like Ja Rule and Lil Mo'.

I hope when all the tears have stopped falling you feel so much better than before and during your time of releasing. Kiss the babies on the forehead, tell them you love them, hug them and take a nap or go play, bake and eat some good food. Be Happy, Be Love, Be What you were missing, and what you needed and wanted within those tears.

Day 63

Hurdles will always be present when all you want to do is be great. You pushed a whole human being out of yourself or had one cut out of you.

If you can do that then Mommy you better jump those hurdles like they are the least worry in your life!

Focus on the finish line. The celebration of completing the challenge. Growing beyond measure and being strong enough to not give up on yourself.

Day 64

One day you just decide it isn't worth losing your mind because they cry.

**Cry my babies cry, let it ALL THE WAY
OUT! Tomorrow will be better because
crying is healing.**

Tough love at an early age is important when you truly want your children to be successful in this beautiful world with some troubled souls.

**Show them tears are okay, (not all the time) they
help you feel better.**

Day 65

Potty Training,
oh the joys and patience one must have.

There isn't a timeline on how much help one dedicates or gives to you. Especially if they are a loved one to the baby/babies.

There should be no question when it comes to helping raise a baby, help should be given at all times not select times. Don't even question it, just do it like nike lolbs.

Everyone has to, needs to and should be on the same page in order for raising little people to be successful.

Day 66

There's so much power in silence and so much strength in noise.

As a woman and a mother we are more than able and capable of handling ourselves and everyone else in these situations and more.

Yeah I know you know right so why mention this then!? Sister Girl Honey Child Listen I'm mentioning it because you need a reminder that in these times you operate at your best! You make shit happen! Although it shouldn't get to this point in order for things to happen. But unfortunately it does and I need you and myself to remember that you are a phenomenal beast sis!

Celebrate how strong you are in silence because that's where we find our power to carry on. Announce how strong you are for being able to shake and move through all the chaos life brings. Because this is what makes us so unfucking stoppable.

Day 67

Sooooo sometimes your schedule gets thrown off because someone else decides to interfere with what you have going on. Sometimes it's life that interferes with your schedule. Things happen, shit happens. Yup it happened to me!

Finally we are getting into a routine and a schedule, and then poof! Something and someone came along and disrupted the flow in the ocean. It was unnerving and annoying but let me share what I learned.

BREATHE!

Just breathe through it all and keep going as you would normally do. The circus won't cancel the show because one act isn't able to perform!

Day 68

When will the words come out instead of the yelling because the words aren't coming out!
The growing pains of an infant/toddler affect both the child and the parent and those around.

EVERYONE IS FRUSTRATED!

Talk, cry, yell, repeat!
You Know What!
Okay let's just talk about everything we're doing so your vocabulary increases and more words start to form!
I know teaching a child to talk is not an easy task but it is well worth all the troubles, trials, tribulations, and more.
Take what I've earned and call it a lesson learned.
Repetition is key in teaching anyone and everyone something. You learn it the more you do it. If you aren't using your leg muscles then eventually you won't be doing much if any walking. It's the same way with teaching a baby to talk and learn over all. Keep doing it until they get and start doing it themselves and don't stop teaching, and guiding until they do what you've been teaching and guiding them to do.

Day 69

Get moving mommy!

It's time to move yourself and things around including baby!

The more energy you burn the better you feel and rest by the end of the night. Baby also may rest better at night as well.

Will they cry?

Of course!

But they will get used to the movement as long as you are consistent and don't lose yourself in adding or doing more to make life better for you and them. Move the energy in your home, the energy around your home, your energy of people and relationships. Everything requires cleaning and releasing. We grow out things, people, and places. So instead of torturing yourself in the long run. Start shifting the energy yourself. Create the change and the growth. If you aren't too familiar with feng shui then research it and see how you can apply it to your life. You can even incorporate some religious ways of living into your life. All of these things and more help move the energy inside of you and outside of you. Around and about you is included.

Day 70

Today we found out how important a schedule is. DoJo wanted to nap at 12 noon because he had gotten up early. Nope! Sir you need to stay awake because nap time is at 2:30.

It was his first day at the library too! Sometimes you have to listen to the baby's body and sometimes you have to listen to mommy's intuition and mommy knows best when it comes to intuition. You can even cancel events that are not as important as others to help tame the offset day. Things like this will happen. It's okay everyone has off days, our bodies could be craving something different.

Day 71

Just go slow mommy no need to rush you're a mother for life now. 👀

That hit me lolbs
Yup read it again cause I felt the same way as I wrote it.

A Mommy For Life......

Day 72

Every ounce of love you give to your baby you are able to give to yourself. That is such a beautiful love to share with yourself and your baby, it's the bond that can't and shouldn't ever be challenged or broken.

Day 73

Get out and be an adult! Be you!
You're so much more than just a mommy.

Get cute, sexy, comfortable, whatever and however go have fun and talk to more adults. Even if it is strangers. Just don't talk about your babies while you're out and don't have baby stuff coming out of your purse lol. Shit happens man and sometimes when all you know is mommy life hell that's all you know is mommy life. I was or at least used to be one of those moms that didn't care. I love my babies and I would sing it at the mountain tops, standing on top of a plane flying in the sky if I could. Then I got tired of people looking at me and my ex husband and ex fiance telling me that all I talk about is my children. At first I was like so what? Who cares? I'm a mom and I love being a mom. Then I realized that people who didn't have children had things in common with them but the level of interest and excitement was gone. I had to figure out and remember what all Shantay did and didn't like and work from there. It was and wasn't fun. It's a journey that's worth traveling, that's for sure. Because sis, look at you, Look at who you didn't know you were, who you truly are inside and out.

Day 74

Other than being a woman, being a mommy is the absolute best fucking thing in the world ever! I mean who else and what else in human life can create and birth another little human!?

That's some more than just outstanding shit.

Being a mommy shows how skilled you are at teaching, nurturing, listening, understanding, loving, and hell taking care of someone who can't even communicate with you. How well trusted and desired you are. Being a mommy is peaceful and full of joy oozing out of your spirit. It's substance and purpose, will power and magick, mystical and mythical.

The laughter, the 10 little toes and fingers, the little boy rolls, the baby! Then when they learn to walk and run and play and talk it's so magickal I can't even begin to describe. A baby's laughter can lighten up just about any person's soul. A baby's presence can bring forth the light of life. The smell of a baby and so much more. I can talk forever and forever about babies and their strength, their will power, their determination, their transforming abilities. The love they have inside of them, the trust they provide and receive without expectation. Babies are the best at teaching us how to love and trust newness. Elders are the best at teaching us how to love and trust after all the trials of life.

Be happy, play, laugh, have fun, get messy, dirty and silly. Create and destroy, build and start over. Just enjoy and have fun. You only get to live this life once. You only get to be their mommy once.

Day 75

Don't forget how to be an adult!

Don't forget how to hold adult conversations

Don't forget that there is a life outside of you being a mother!

Don't forget that you matter

Don't forget that your smile is meant for you just like it is meant for others.

Don't forget that you are a woman with a dream, a woman with inspiration and goals to achieve.

Don't forget that you are life, you carry life, you create life, life is you!

Don't forget your value, how much you give out and how little you get in return. Change That!

Don't forget what you've been through to get where you are.

Don't forget your power, your grace, your beauty, your magick ...

Don't forget who the fuck you ARE!

Day 76

Rest when it's time to rest!

You have your entire life ahead of you, being a mommy is not going anywhere lol seriously.

I know if I don't do it no one will do it and it will never get done. Or it will be half assed.

So what! Who cares!

They don't care and some of them do care. The point is to stop and breathe sometimes. The only way that truly happens is by you putting yourself first for a moment. Just for a moment.

Day 77

Okay yes I talked about crying a couple of times. Yes, I'm going to talk about it again!

Why because there is absolutely no reason a child should just cry and cry and cry about every single thing and for every single reason or opportunity they can cry.

USE YOUR WORDS! That means you have to talk as much as you want the baby/babies to talk

The more you pacify the child from learning the more you are enabling the child to live under you versus going out into the real world. Yes they are babies but they are learning and the funny thing is they WANT to learn. They want to do and go and grow and more. They can't speak so they cry. They get frustrated so they cry, they have emotions in general and don't know how to express or communicate anything other than crying it out. Even when there isn't anything to cry about, the best way to communicate it is to just cry.

Let them cry and when they're finished talk about it. I've learned and I'm currently learning that words, pictures, and movement are the best forms of communication for baby to mom, dad, siblings or those who can talk. The more you expose your baby to words, emotions and behaviors of how to express themselves, the faster the communication barriers lift and the crying subsides. Even with the beginning phases of learning to talk there will still be crying because so much new stuff is coming in it's almost like system overload. So they cry some more. The one other language babies understand or inner stand is laughter, hugs, and smiling. I've learned that sometimes they just need, and want random and on demand hugs, laughter, and smiles just like older children and adults do. Sit down with them, write some words out, draw some happy, sad, and angry faces with them so they learn to at least point at how they feel. Sign language helps a lot as well. I started implementing rubbing my stomach or pointing to my mouth so they can let me know they are hungry and thirsty. I know babies wanna eat every couple of hours, but in reality honey you lose track of time and when the crying begins you have to stop, think and check the time and remember what happened a couple of hours ago. Then you have to go through your other memory bank of figuring out why they're crying and that includes pure communication. Are you hungry, thirsty, cold, hot, bored, sleepy, do you need a diaper changed, are you sad, happy, trying to figure out how to play with a toy, are you emotional right now, etc. Even this can become frustrating for both you and baby until you figure out what the crying is for you have to stay calm. Once you figure it out, share a hug, a smile, a congratulations, good job mommy and baby you did it. You did it together!

**They're counting on you and believe it or not
you're counting on them too.**

Day 78

Some days are just what they are mommy and the best thing for any mommy to do is get through them because it will only last as long as you allow it to!

Do what needs to be done, say what needs to be said, feel what needs to be felt and then exhale and let it go.

My ritual for these types of days is as follows:

- Clean up the house and have everyone pitch in even if it's just straightening up,

- Like an oven range light on or the refrigerator light on, some dim light in the area of the house that has been cleaned and put to sleep.

- Put all the children to sleep and that includes daddy too (lol).

- Grab some essential oils, an incense, a diffuser, something that emits a good aroma in the air and light it, burn it, spray it, project it into the air on all levels and areas of your home,

- If you like candle lit baths/showers then light some damn candles in your bathroom and bedroom so you don't have to turn on the lights afterwards. Grab whatever pajamas you'll be wearing prior to turning out the lights, all your necessities prior to getting in the bath/shower and prior to turning out the lights.

The goal is to make as little noise as possible when you get out of your bath/shower so you dedicate time to yourself without being disturbed or disturbing others.

- Some people like music in the shower/bath just don't have it loud our belt singing lol

- Some people like bath bombs and oils in their water/ shower. Gather all that you like or all that your intuition leads you to grab. Some of my favorites for a bath are lavender, rosemary, orange, lemongrass, frankincense, and myrrh. I have some handmade ones like ancestor oils, personal power oils, self love oils, and enlightenment oils. It depends on my mood and my intention which one I use. Some calm you down and some lift you up, some heal you, some give you insight, some give you the power you lost somewhere throughout the day.

- Sometimes I add flowers in my bath or eucalyptus in the shower. Brush your teeth before you get in the shower. Wash with your favorite healthy washes and if it ain't wednesday, don't wash your hair but you most certainly can give it a good rinse. That helps release the mental stress. Using a good leave-in conditioner helps because you can massage it into your tresses and open up your hair follicles for growth and releasing/healing. If you need to shave then shave (waxing is better, painful, but better)

- When you get out of the shower, don't rub yourself dry, pat yourself dry. Take a good look at yourself in the mirror and acknowledge how sexy and dope you are fresh out the shower! Glistening wet has a nice twinkle to it. Some like to air dry, hopefully you have a comfy place to just sit and dry or lay and dry. Don't dry to the point where your skin feels like it's tightening or cracking.

- Now grab those oils or body butter and lather and rub, massage yourself in ways that feel good and with intentions. For me rubbing down helps push those pent up emotions down and out my feet. Rubbing up helps pull those good emotions to a higher level and it elevates my being overall. Whatever I use I always top it off with coconut oil to seal in the moisture and put my socks or clothes on right away to help lock in the moisture more and the scent has to be on point too! I like to smell a certain way depending on what I'm tending to in my mind, body, emotions, and spirit.

- Comb and oil your scalp, use your good bonnet, not the one that's beat up lol.

- Write in your journal, meditate, or just sit in the quietness with a candle lit or a dim light and just take in the aroma of whatever scent you put in the house before you showered. When you feel yourself drifting to a happy place, know that sleep is next and the best part of this all is you have dismissed your stress and the worry of the day.

PS: Before I put my clothes on I always, always, always, admire my body in the mirror no matter how I think it looks or the comments others have said about my body and in this case your body. Love on your body because it is YOUR body and it's awesome as fuck sis/bro cause men/daddies need this type of love too. Hell if you love on yourself enough you might excite yourself and please yourself or start a good session with your partner, who knows. And yes this is a ritual you and your mate can do together so don't feel like it's something you "have" to do on your own. Love is to be cherished but shared at the same time and babyyyyy let me be the one to tell you that sharing this form of love(once you have given it to yourself) is the absolute best because the connection is ultimately so powerful when the male and feminine energies are combined both inward and outward.

Shhhhhh Rest well you deserve and look forward to waking up feeling yourself!

Day 79

The adventures of the traveling infant/toddler that was once okay with taking risks then became afraid and now he's back to being the confident daredevil. Go to sleep DoJo, lay down DoJo, don't you get off of the couch anymore DoJo. It never ends and it becomes frustrating and you can sometimes lose your patience with a child that doesn't want to listen and then smiles at you softening your heart. It's a gift and a curse all at once, and the best thing you can do is just breathe and stay in constant repetition.

Eventually you will defeat your battle of the traveling infant/toddler blues.

Look at it as a way to play the listening game, or play follow the leader. Maybe even a healthy game of resting in some sorts.

The point is don't lose your cool, your patience, or your ability to stand firm on your discipline which is so vitally important at this age.

Even people this small will test you and push you out of your comfort zone.

Don't back down now!

Have fun with it and be stern. A child doesn't matter; the age will always see how far they can go and what their limits are. You have to know your limits even when they put their charm on you. I've learned through all of my children and parenting days that the more fun you have and implement with learning the better it is for the child, childre, baby, or babies to learn. Learning doesn't have to be strict to the point of no love and laughter being included. How in the hell d o you teach and discipline with fun? In all honesty there's no blueprint for this at all. Some may even beg to differ that you cannot discipline with love and laughter and maybe myself and my father are special individuals because he disciplined me with love and a smile and fun. WE played and had fun and when it was time to stop he would always hug me with a smile and firmly say okay that's enough we're done now. Sometimes I would test him and just like any other black parent my middle name was called and that meant it was really done lol. You have it in you, just tap in and manage the power you already possess.

Day 80

Trust someone with your babies so you can peacefully take a break!

Listen closely when I say that taking a break "AWAY" from your children/babies is more than wanted, needed, and necessary! You absolutely MUST take a step away. I know, I Know.....

I'm going to miss him/her, can I trust so and so to tend to them, will he/she be okay for x amount of time that I am away. OMGoodness I have to pump while my baby is away and the list of why you can't step away will continue to grow as long as you stand there and actually THINK of reasons to stay. I've come to the conclusion that mothers have separation anxiety more than the babies do!

Stop it, that's nonsense. I hear some of you saying as I share this small moment with you.

But the truth is we actually do! Guess what!? It's more than just okay! It's actually healthy if you ask me. I would be more worried and concerned if you didn't have separation anxiety, to me that says you love your baby, you protect your baby, and if those are the small simple things that keep you sane about the life quality for your baby then so be it.

What I will say is start small if you have this hurdle to overcome. That small step could simply mean, being in another room for 10-

15 minutes giving yourself some much needed space while someone else tends to the baby. Then gradually taking more and more time until you can actually go a day or two without your baby. Because let's face it, we ALL need and want to go on adult vacations and how can we if separation anxiety is keeping us tied to baby versus baby being tied to us?

So take your time; Peacefully. Step by step, moment by moment it will happen.

Day 81

Piggy backing off of yesterday ......

I miss my baby!

Do I miss his mischievous behavior? Hell no I do not. Do I miss his smile and his laughter, and all the other cute little things he does like he's doing now? Hell yeah!

I even miss when he does something bad and I reprimand him and he smiles to try and win me over from being disciplined. That's what children do right.

But overall I miss my baby!

Some people will say you are crazy and they've only been gone for a moment.

Don't let them affect you! You're their mother, you carried them all your life, yes all of your life. So in reality a part of you is missing and needs to be reconnected.

Fuck these types of people and go get your baby (once your me-time is over), go love on your baby and welcome your baby home with love, smiles, kisses, and open arms. Who cares if they all think you're crazy and even if you feel crazy for having the ups and downs of being a parent. It's perfectly okay.

What I like to do when I have my time away is:

- First enjoy my me-time.

- I have a moment of silence and start prepping myself and whatever environment my babies will be coming into when they return to me. It builds excitement and it makes the welcome more warm and loving.

- Another thing I do is keep in touch with who they are with and how their day is going. Sometimes, "sometimes, I talk to them throughout the time they are away, especially if they are not having a good time away.

- Welcome them with a smile, and open arms.

One thing I want you to know is you and your baby/babies will never know what being missed is if you are never away from each other. The saying out of sight, out of mind is not always true. Sometimes out of sight means you're on my mind.

Day 82

I just want both hands and my lap to be free

Yup it's a damn rollercoaster! One minute I want to be all on them and the next get off of me. My, oh my what bad behavior and example I am setting for them. What I do to them they will do to me and others. I mention this because sometimes, hell most times we don't even realize exactly what we're doing to ourselves let alone others.

So if you ever wondered why your baby/babies, children do certain things, I beg of you to take a moment and look at yourself. What exactly are you teaching them and how are you treating them to treat yourself and others? How will they treat themselves based on what you've shown them?

I'm not bashing you at all because that would mean I need to bash myself and that I will not do. What I Am challenging you to do is be mindful of the love and behavior you display and give so that you are aware of the type of love you will notice and receive in return.

Babies only know how to be happy and sad. They don't know much of any other emotions in between those two. It takes time to build those other emotions. They build those other emotions based off of the person they know emotions from the most, and that is mommy. It's mommy because although daddy planted the seed (yes he plays a major role in their character, personality and overall being just like you do) because you carried and nurtured your baby since you were in your mother's womb. Once you became pregnant with that particular baby you began sharing and giving up yourself to give and provide life for your baby. So for the first approximate 5years of life your baby will look primarily to you for just about everything. Even if they have another favorite person they still will look right at you. So feel free to be you but also be mindful of the authentic you that you are giving and sharing with the world and your baby/babies.

Day 83

Embracing motherhood on multiple levels!

People think it's no big deal to be a breastfeeding mother, a mother to an infant/toddler and a mother of teens and be a working mom, and/or a business mom/entrepreneur. Let me tell you it is so vital that you have a sisterhood and some form, shape, or fashion of support.

It's detrimental to your health in all capacities to have support from every angle possible!

Being the outstanding mother that I Am, I operate on multiple, multiple levels of life. I found myself being happy again to actually be able to produce more than enough breast milk for my newborn daughter while I Am away from her. Business never stops and neither does mothering. In the midst of it all I found the courage, the confidence, the strength, and self-love to take myself into my own love and arms and put myself on a pedestal.

Because I did that!

I rock at being a business mom, I rock being myself, and I rock it all mentally, spiritually, physically, emotionally, and I looked effortlessly show stopping while doing it!

Hell yeah I have underlying issues, as we all do! But that does not and should not stop you from shining ever so brightly as you are meant to!

Can You Say Woman Of Life

Day 84

Rest and Reset!

Being a business mommy I have to be away from my babies from time to time. Today happened to be one of those days that I was away from them for pretty much the entire day! Man when I tell you they don't take kindly to these days. I feel so bad for them and the person keeping them for me. They cry for hours on end. DoJo misbehaves because he hasn't learned to say I miss mommy (He calls me BahBah). SisSea refuses to stop crying or drink breast milk from a bottle. Before you say it, Yes, I started her on the bottle early for this very purpose, but that little girl is smart beyond her months lolbs. So when the smoke clears and mommy is back home to them and then back home to me. We all are exhausted and clingy and we just lounge while cuddling.

I must say that these are some of the best moments a mother can have or ask for. I love my babies beyond words and this realm. I'm so grateful for their spirits and their ability to speak to me without their words. For my ability to connect and speak to them. To inner-stand and over stand what they have to say before they can actually say it.

The mothering bond comes naturally when you take a moment to just stop and breathe.

When you take a moment to stop letting your mind and emotions carry you away because your baby is crying and decide to just focus on the energy and feel yourself be guided to nurture the part or parts your baby needs some TLC on. This bond is potent whether it is you near each other or far away. Yes there will be and are times you will hear your baby cry when you are miles apart. Yes they are time you will hear and know your baby is saying Ma'Ma'. Overall you will hear and know your baby is speaking to you. No you're not crazy and no you don't have to go running to your baby unless there's danger or your intuition tells you that you need to. Otherwise a quick check-in will be sufficient to help ease your heart, mind and soul.

Day 85

Sometimes you have to not worry about cleaning up and you have to not let the clinginess get to you!

Yes, we rested and we were supposed to be resetting too. But that doesn't mean that the mess didn't happen. That's when a mess really happens lol. No one cares about the mess when it's being made unless you're focused on everything except the moment that is creating the mess if you pick up what I'm putting down (point intended)!

The point being made here is leave the mess sometimes and finish restoring and resetting before you hop back into the daily duties of being a mommy. You know, clean up, feed the babies, nap time, clean up again, dinner, bath time, clean up again. Sometimes you just have to leave it there all day and clean up once or wait and clean up the next day. After all, the mess will be made over and over, again and again.

The lesson will present itself over and over until you learn what's meant to be learned. Going into more deeper mental and spiritual/wisdom aspects. Sometimes you can learn the lesson and still repeat the learning process just so that you are picking up on the things you didn't notice before. As an adult, woman, mother, sister, aunt, niece, cousin, friend, ex-wife, etc. I have learned that there are new lessons within the same lesson. Whatever the case may be for you, use it all to your advantage and make the most/best of everything you face and experience in life.

Tomorrow is a brand new day and the mess will be there regardless.

Day 86

😭*I don't like the way I look at all!*

Every child I have I get smaller and smaller. I'm already a small person with a use to be small, thick frame. Now I'm just boobs! Yes it's only 3 months, yes I'm breastfeeding, no I don't get to eat a lot, I barely get to exercise (because these blues are a fucking rollercoaster)! Because I'm by myself with two little babies all the damn time. Because they both want to be loved on and cuddled. Because I wanted to be loved on and cuddled when I was pregnant with both of them. Because affection was and still is so important to me and to them as well.

Aaahhhhhhhh! I DON'T CARE if people think having a small frame is sexy. I'm not happy or comfortable in my own skin/body!

I'll get to where I'm happy and comfortable, I know it will take time and patience. Determination and work, to stop breastfeeding, to eat properly, but right now! I'm growing through it all moment by moment. Hell by each piece of clothing I grab and I get upset with, I Am Growing. It hurts but growth is never comfortable or energizing. Even when we don't feel the growth we need to rest so our body can grow. With that being said can these babies take a nap for once and sleep like other babies sleep for naps. Please please pretty please DoJo and SisSea take a real nap.

I accept myself for all of what I am, who I am and how I look. Which isn't completely bad, just not appealing to me.

Small & curvy loading . . .

Day 87

Today we will just sit here.

No bad feelings, no bad vibes. No negative emotions, no fighting to get things done.

There's a time and a place for everything and everyone
Ecclesiastes 3:11

Remember you are a virtuous woman and being a virtuous woman means you've done and still all of the above and more.

Be Still in the midst of it all. Enjoy everything that you don't normally get to pay attention to.

Day 88

The sunshine

Good food

Happy comfy clothes

Being around loved ones

Great conversations

Is all you need on most days, it seems to wash all of the bad away and you forget what bad came your way that day.

Go and Be in that circle, that environment, that love and energy.

Day 89

Hearing my baby cry is soul wrenching! Especially when you know all they want is mommy. Nothing is wrong and no one is hurting them, all they want is mommy.

Yup I have a hard time NOT giving in and swooping my baby up. I don't understand nor do I inner stand why or how a mother or father can just let their babies cry. Now don't get me wrong some days I will let her and him, them both get it out of their system. But for the most part if my babies cry you better believe I'm not far away and if I Am, I'm on the phone or I can feel them crying. I can hear them and I know they want mommy.

But what I also want to share with you is sometimes we do have to let our baby cry. It's soooooo hard to hear it and not do something about it. It's sooooo hard to just hear it. It's just hard!

I'm working on it and I Am learning that even though your baby can and will cry it doesn't mean I have to run and jump every single time. Allow them some time to regain composure and find ways to calm themselves. Self soothing is vitally important because the more we run to their beckon call the more we are telling them and showing them that we will save them from everything and everyone. That we have the answer to everything. The truth is we don't have the answer to everything even though most times Momma knows best we still don't know everything. We absolutely cannot save them from everyone and everything. Yes that's Momma's baby but truthfully, Momma's baby is simply us raising adults. That means one day Momma won't be there to rescue her big ole grown ass baby, they have to grow up, they cannot stay babies forever. So allow yourself to let your baby learn themselves as they grow throughout their life. Save yourself the future stress, headache and spare your life because stressing over these soon to be adult babies of ours will kill you, no jokes. Knowing that we want to always swoop our babies up, we have to discipline ourselves to teach them how to be independent and when to be dependent. Because life calls for both aspects. Doing so helps us to know that we live, to live for them, once we live to live for ourselves.

If you want to be a part of their life experiences then you will allow them to grow and keep yourself alive in the process.

Day 90

Just chill!

We're tired mommy and we want a nap! Can we all just lay on you and rest!? Absolutely you sure can.

These are the days that we all wish for, the moments when less means so much more. We don't have to do a thang at all (Dru-Hill singing in my head lol). We can just take our time and lay here and talk and eat and sleep and Love, Be at Peace, Be the Peace.

Today I had that very pleasure of just embracing my babies sleeping in my arms, next to me, laying their head on my lap. It was just so magickal and it made me so damn happy I wanted to cry! I held back the tears because I didn't want to wake them by sucking up the snotty boogers from the tears flowing. I don't need a drawn out page of info.

Remember: "the moments when <u>less </u>means so much more!"

I Love You My Babies!

Day 91

I've come to the conclusion that babies, well my babies will never have a consistent schedule. No matter what I do or how I do it they are them and that's perfectly okay. I would like to be more organized with them as I keep talking. I want them to interact with other people, places, things, and babies. Maybe I want something for them that they just aren't ready for. Because we can't seem to make it outside ever on a good weathered day!

Let's talk about the different personalities and how one affects the other! One is crying and the other is happy. One is sleeping, the other is awake! One is ready to do and go and the other is like nah I'm chilling. They are complete night and day babies so how in the world does a mother work this?

Conclusion Just work with what you have and don't push it or them to be something they are not. Don't give up on them either. Sometimes they don't understand the purpose until they get the experience and the experience can mean repetition. Sometimes it can simply mean finding their groove. New babies back to back is a challenge that's worth facing. They learn, you learn and you all learn together. Trust the process of growth.

Day 92

The best advice I have for you today (speaking to myself as well) is to get up before they do and do something for you before you do anything for anyone else!

Start a routine, a ritual, do something for you and you only and that includes not being on social media, answering texts, emails, messages and more. This time is strictly for you!

At night take some time for yourself to actually clear the day away, prep for tomorrow and then to finally just drift off into the sandman's land.

I'm sure there are things you wish you could have the time to do. Take the time, make the time, the time is now to do what you want and need. To do what you desire to do for you. So you can and will be of better love and service to yourself and the babies.

There should never ever be a reason you don't stop and do for you because if it wasn't for you there wouldn't be a them!

You matter, woman!

You matter mommy!

Day 93

Put a little bit of self~love in your daily life!

If you do nothing else at all for yourself as a woman, (who is the most extravagant being on the planet), as a mother then stop and give yourself a hug! Do something that makes you happy. Even if that means saying fuck it I'll get to it later. Do just that and remember to smile.

Today I sat Indian style and listened to music, danced as I sat and wrote in my journal

Things to accomplish, Goals to achieve, Dreams to fulfill Life to live and to share with special people Today I smiled as I wrote and gazed at my future

Today I smiled just for myself.

Smiling for me means I smile for them and they smile in general.

Day 94

Heart Wrenching, hurt, and fear that something will happen to my child.

See I'm not just a mother of an infant and pre-toddler, I have teenagers as well!

For some they don't have to worry about much happening to their baby, child, children. For me and other mothers like me. Brown and Black mothers, we have to worry before we conceive. I don't want anything to happen to my baby, my child. You see, WE don't get that extra TLC that other women get.

Yes, I do mean Caucasian women. This isn't to bash or shame anyone. This is stating facts!

A brown or black woman alone is not cared for and when she becomes pregnant the care diminishes even further. WE are misdiagnosed on purpose. We are told to be strong. We can do this because we're always strong. Our lives have no value because some of you are intimidated by us. It's sad! It's hurtful! It's painful! It's SCARY AS HELL, to know that just because of the color of my skin, the value of my life and my unborn/born child/children's life is not nurtured and cared for the same. Or at all for that matter.

I'm not saying Caucasian women don't get mistreated, I'm stating that women of melanin get mistreated more and at a higher rate. All of this came to me due to the facts in daily prenatal life and birthing rates in the United States as a whole. But what really puts me in a state of exhaustion and anger is my children having to be mindful of how they move and speak and are seen in public. Last night I feared my son's life and I still currently fear for all of my children's lives. I'm afraid to let him go outside, but I have to allow him to move, live, and be free.

I refuse to let the color of his skin and his culture keep him from living freely in every way imaginable.

Hold your babies, hug your babies, love your babies!

Enjoy and embrace every particle and speckle of them. Nothing is permanent.

Day 95

Man when I tell you I struggled to feel good and confidently know I look good today!

I'm a small lady like I stated before so most people will be like girl, you are crazy!

You look amazing to have just given birth to a baby. I'll tell all of you the exact same thing I told my last two children's father..... Heavy is not the only uncomfortable/unpleasant body size!

I've never been so tiny and what I see as disproportioned in my life. I can't gain weight and right now if I do it all goes to the wrong places. I cried by myself to myself as I thought about how I looked in the mirror. It isn't just my body, it's my skin and my face too! I don't feel that healthy vibrant after birth glow going on nor do I see it. This is the second time in my 5 after birth experiences that I have not been happy with how I look. I know it takes time and I have to be honest and say my bounce back has always been superb so I'm pretty sure I'm over evaluating things. I just want my clothes to fit (meaning I want to fill them up again), I want them to look right on me. I want to see my curves again, I want to feel beautiful, look sexy, and be very confident in whatever I put on whenever I put it on.

My goal?

When this weather gets right, I will be outside with both babies everyday pushing myself and working my babies to be the best they can be mentally, physically, emotionally, and spiritually.

Until then, I Am not giving up. Exercising in the house and in my garage.

Confidence can be so hard to hold on to when your eyes see what does NOT make you happy. What a lot of people fail to realize is that our eyes tell our minds what to think and our minds tell our heart what to feel. Our heart tells our throats what to speak. With that being said perception is everything and what you see is what you get! You have to add some discernment within your perception in order to gauge the feelings that come from those thoughts. I've talked about me being unhappy with the way I look pretty close together. As if something would change so swiftly over night. The truth of the matter is I wish something would change for the better overnight. A lot of other shit seems to happen overnight so where the fuck is my weight gain in all the right places over night? Giving birth and being happy with the way you look afterwards is and can be one of the most difficult things a woman can face. What the fuck happened to me!? That's what most women think after giving birth and seeing themselves in the mirror. It ain't much of anything tight and firm or fit as it used to be. The fastest weight loss happens from giving birth. It took 9-10 months to gain all the extra weight needed for creating a small human in your uterus. Then once your body releases your baby and placenta you lose like 15 pounds. Depending on your body hell you could lose more. I'm mentioning and sharing this information because one a lot of folks don't know. Two I'll be the reminder for those who do know and may have forgotten. Three Knowing these things help us all decipher what the hell and how the hell did this happen to me and what the hell do I have to do and need to do to make the most and best out of this unpleasant but meaningful change that has taken place in my mind, body, heart, and soul.

Find something about yourself that gives a speckle of confidence to move forward and be well. Be one with your physical being like you are one with your baby and how you are one with being a mother. Becoming a mother is what made you lose the body confidence you had in the first place and I'm not bringing this to the forefront of your mind to make you feel like shit. I'm bringing it forward so that you can remember all of those days and nights you were so happy to be becoming a mommy.

Day 96

Okay, I know, he is still little and she is still new, but my goodness is the "I miss mommy thing," going to be the reason they can't stay with other people and I can't get away momentarily?

I don't know, but what I do know is it hurts me to leave them and to leave them with anyone while they're crying and only wanting me. It makes it hard to go back out into the world and be Shantay. It makes it hard to leave them with people, it makes it hard to focus on why I had to leave in the first place. My feelings are hurt because they're crying until I return. My boobs hurt because I breastfeed SisSea (even when I pump they still hurt). I don't know if many of you know but when you're a breastfeeding mother and your baby cries for you your boobs hurt like hell. It's the connection that holds you close to them and dear to them. It's loving your babies from a distance. It's loving unconditionally.

All the babies want is mommy because she is safe, she is love, she is happy, she is home to the baby.

I know this can be stressful and frustrating. Some people may even feel like you're wrong for wanting to be away from your baby. But the truth is your soul and your spirit need to be fed just as much as theirs and even more because you, my sister, are spreading yourself among others. It's okay to step away, it's okay to be you, it's okay to leave and come back.

It's okay to not mommy for just a moment.

Day 97

*I wanna go outside already,
I'm tired of being in the house!*

Listen! Me and DoJo are tired of these walls and SisSea is ready to move around. We hear the birds chirping, we see the sun shining, we hear and feel the wind blowing and the trees swaying their naked branches.

WE WANNA GO OUTSIDE, BUT DAMMIT IT'S STILL NOT THAT WARM FOR SisSea!

Every time we go out, she shivers and shrivels up lol. She loses her breath from the wind blowing and then ultimately she begins crying. Then DoJo cries because she's crying (insert facial expression here particularly a nice face palm). I've tried warmer clothes and blankets and such, but yeah it only lasts for about 15-30 minutes. So I guess I have to take it in spurts and be patient with her getting used to the weather. What I did incorporate is just opening the windows on the house sometimes, opening the front door and sitting on the porch so that we can go right back inside if she gets too cold too fast. It's helping her, however me and DoJo wanna run and walk and play lol. We go outside in the front while she's sleeping, and then he needs a nap.

The day to go outside and take a good brisk walk, jog, run is upon me and when I tell you I can't wait for that day! I cannot wait for that day at all! I'm searching for the right 2 seat stroller.

Yes, I'm excited lol See you outside one day soon!

Nature feeds a postpartum mother because nature is a mother naturally.

Day 98

As a mother for the 5th time around I absolutely love getting lost in the moments that I spend with my children/babies. Just shutting the world out sometimes makes all the difference.

Today Me and DoJo ran and walked up and down the sidewalk barefoot. It was cool but not too cold and not too hot.

As long as we didn't stand in the shade and catch a draft or gust of the wind we were good. The sun shined just enough to keep us warm without a coat or socks and shoes on our feet. He enjoyed being out there and probably as much if not more than I did. I was just embracing his smile and his laughter. His curiosity to explore more of the outside and go on adventures into places he hasn't been. I actually enjoy him crying to stay outside. I don't wanna go back in either DoJo, but we have to for SisSea, and we have to because it's going to get cold.

We worked together, we ate together, we played together, we took a quick nap together, and We smiled together. These are the moments that steal my heart away and the moments that I'll miss out on everything that is going on in the world.

Moments like these last for more than a lifetime

I Love Being a Mommy

Day 99

Today we just slept, well at least me and SisSea slept lol. DoJo wanted to run, cry, scream, jump kick, shout and who knows what else. It was rainy and for some reason we needed that rest. For some reason I needed to release everything I have been holding onto and just feel both the good and the bad inside of me. I needed to just be humble, be grateful, and be silent, be unseen.

I needed both the inner and outward versions of me.

Balance mommy, because every step of this journey requires both your good and bad sides.

The good to attract, reflect, project, reciprocate, and the bad to protect all that I Am and all that my children are.

There will not be a single moment in the rest of your life and entire being that you will not move and do what you do for your children to the extent that you do for you and your children. Now it may excite you, it may encourage you to pursue more. It may even enhance you but the choice, the decisions you make will be based on what is best for you as a woman and mother ultimately meaning what is best for your child/children.

Always live, learn, and let go, so that you may continue to be the best version of yourself so you will be the best mother throughout it all.

You live on even when you are gone.

Your children and children's, children will carry you forward and more.

Day 100

Whatever you do, just be you from your core and be the best mommy you could ever imagine having and being. Be the mommy your children see and believe in you being. Listen to your babies both now and later because they will forever be yours, you're a mommy because of them and only they can mold and shape you into being the best mommy for them ever. You just have to actively listen and execute the task of being their mother. They have unimaginable growth, growth so strong and consistent because their mommy is so strong and consistent.

I'm sharing my rollercoaster ride with you because every womb wound needs attention in different ways and manners. Being left alone to care for two small babies on your own is a challenge and it's simple all at once. It's simple because I've been down this road before but this time I had more on my plate than what I had prior to. This time the help I had in the past is not available in my present. This time all I wanted was help from daddy and daddy alone. I didn't get what I wanted and that hurt like hell. I didn't get what I needed on this end of the spectrum because it wasn't high up on the list. I got what I needed. But after giving birth and almost losing my life in the process, I've learned a new level of self love and respect. You see you have to give and love you the way you want others to give and love on you. It doesn't mean there will never be a bad day. It simply means that within all of the greatness chaos still thrives. How you handle that chaos and how you tend to the wounds once the battle is won determines how you move forward and what lessons will you apply to not be stuck in the same place. Day 100 is me moving forward. It's me claiming my newfound power. It's me stepping into the realm of life I thought I would know no matter what came my way, love to know and live happily with peace, love, light and life.

PS: I wanted you all to know that the reason you see the repetition within my story is because not much of anything that we face changes over night. Not only that, this is a different level of healing and womb wounds take a while to heal. Eating helps your diet and so does exercise. You have to help yourself heal and the only thing to do is to release what's got you dis-eased in the first place. Figuring out what's making you hold on to unhealthy matters is challenging. That alone can and will take some time getting used to. You may not know what's got you the way you are and furthermore, figuring out who you are now (after giving birth) is challenging. It's meant to make you get it together.

Womb Healing Affirmation

My womb is me and I Am My Womb, Healed, Solely, and Completely. 360 degrees of Life

My womb is a universe of peace, love, light, and life.

My womb brings forth life.

My womb is a portal of the known and unknown.

My womb is safe and sacred

My womb is cherished and adorned with love, gratefulness, and protection.

My womb is powerful enough to heal without restrictions and restraint.

My womb loves me as I love her.

My womb is a warrior and creates with love.

My womb is Love in its purest form.

My womb receives only positive love and energy from the right people, never confusing lust for love and attaching ourselves to the wrong people.

My womb rejects those with the wrong intentions.

ONE WOMB WOUND AT A TIME

My womb is my ancestors, free from pain and struggle.

My womb was meant for me and I Am meant for my womb.

My womb is valuable but also priceless.

My womb houses wisdom and spirituality.

My womb is no longer hurt and angry because of incorrect decisions I've made in my past.

My womb is my garden of life and love. Whatever and Whoever I choose to allow, to plant seeds will grow.

My womb forgives me and I forgive my womb.

My womb is mystically magick.

My womb is an eternal blessing forevermore.

Womb Angel.

Nurturing Mother Affirmations:

I Am my mother's child but I Am Not My Mother.

I am the best version of my children's mother and I allow room for growth.

I Am caring, nurturing, and compassionate.

I love life and life loves me.

I give myself room to fail in order for me to grow and get it right.

I Am happy to be their mother

I Am happy he is their father.

I Am thankful that I am able to provide for my children.

I Am the mother I always dreamed of being.

I Am the mother my children need, want, and deserve for me to be.

I Am an inner-standing mother. I actively listen, while communicating.

I Am happy my children chose me as their mother.

I Am happy that I Am loved as a mother.

I Am open to becoming more than I see myself becoming.

I Am a great teacher and caretaker.

I Am to be trusted as a mother.

I Am grateful to have given birth.

I Am thankful and grateful that I accepted being a mother.

I Am grateful for being able to provide TLC

I Am blessed to look as good as I do having birthed 5 children naturally.

I Am thankful and ask for guidance that the ancestors chose me to break the generational cycles.

Body Confidence Affirmations:

My body loves me and all that I do for it

My body takes care of me nonstop daily. My body is a powerhouse

My body is overflowing with love and light.

My body gives my spirit a home.

My body carries me through life.

My mind, body, and soul are one within.

My mind is open to projecting the best me into the world.

My heart is pure with good intentions

My body healthy

My body is healed

My body is rested and energized.

My body is strong

My body is fit just for me in every way imaginable.

My body is desired and approved of.

I Am worthy

I Am value

I Am Abundance

I Am Show stoppingly gorgeous.

My body holds the answers I seek and love/life I deserve to have.

My body and I are one with Earth, this realm, and this lifetime.

Sexual Healing Affirmations::

My Pussy is Divine

My Pussy is prosperity and abundance.

My Pussy is peace and chaos

My Pussy is calm and serene.

My Pussy is not only powered by sex and creating babies.

My Pussy is happy, warm, and loving.

My Pussy fulfills my desires, dreams, goals and wishes.

My Pussy is healing

My Pussy contains everything I need and want.

My Pussy is creativity at it's finest.

My Pussy adorns her loved ones

My Pussy is My Pussy

My Pussy only connects with the right person.

My Pussy is Power

My Pussy is Home

My Pussy is Family

ONE WOMB WOUND AT A TIME

My Pussy has stability and trust

My Pussy is safe and protected from wrong doings, harm, and
unintentional lovers. My Pussy is balanced

My Pussy is an essential to life

My Pussy is healthy and honorable.

Made in the USA
Columbia, SC
07 October 2022

68602494R00107